THE SUPREME COURT

in the American System of Government

THE GODKIN LECTURES AT HARVARD UNIVERSITY, 1955

Bachrach 1941

THE

SUPREME COURT

in the American System of Government

ROBERT H. JACKSON

Late Associate Justice, Supreme Court
of the United States

HARVARD UNIVERSITY PRESS • CAMBRIDGE • 1957

2943

The Godkin Lectures on the Essentials of Free Government and the Duties of the Citizen were established at Harvard University in memory of Edwin Lawrence Godkin (1831-1902).

FOREWORD

In March 1954 the Harvard Graduate School of Public Administration invited Mr. Justice Jackson to become the Godkin Lecturer for the academic year 1954-55. The Justice accepted and chose as his topic for the three lectures, "The Supreme Court in the American System of Government." February of 1955 was tentatively set as the date for delivery. The Justice began outlining his subject and formulating his ideas soon after he accepted the invitation, and by the end of summer, 1954, he had completed six drafts of the first lecture and two of the second and third. He then reorganized the whole and wrote one more draft of the first two lectures and two partial redrafts of the third.

Mr. Justice Jackson died suddenly on October 9, 1954. He had worked for several hours on the third Godkin lecture the day before his death, and notes indicating further revisions were found in his briefcase after he was stricken.

The Justice had intended to write several more drafts before February. Nevertheless, in view of the substantially completed form of the work, the decision was made to publish what he had already written. Except for technical corrections which the Justice himself would have made before delivery, the lectures remain in the form of the latest drafts to come from his hands. Revision has been limited to grammatical changes and in some places to changes in sentence structure for the sake of clarification. Such revision has been done by the undersigned—the Justice's law clerk, who worked closely with him on the lectures, and the Justice's son, with whom he had discussed his subject matter. Nothing has been added to or deleted from the thought content in any of the three lectures.

Though the Justice had indicated where footnotes were to be added, he had not written all of them himself. Therefore, scattered notes throughout the lectures are not his own. Those which are starred have been supplied. In most instances, the source material for such notes was obvious; in a few, however, a citation was added which seemed to fit most closely the Justice's thought.

This, therefore, is an unfinished, yet substantially completed, work. It is unfinished in the sense that had the Justice lived the final product would have been polished to the perfection which he demanded of himself. It is, however, substantially completed in the sense that it expresses his matured and deep convictions regarding the institution of which he had been so close and keen an observer, first from without and then from within, over the past two decades.

E. BARRETT PRETTYMAN, JR.
WILLIAM ELDRED JACKSON

CONTENTS

THE SUPREME COURT

in the American System of Government

I

THE SUPREME COURT

as a Unit of Government

I N THESE convulsive times, I take your invitation to discuss "The Supreme Court in the American System of Government" as calling for more than a mere compilation of legal citations. It suggests, instead, some reëxamination of the premises of American constitutional democracy, which now is confronted with an armed doctrine claiming to be a newer and higher form of democracy. These rival ideologies clash nowhere more sharply than over the character and functions of a judiciary. It has been our aim, always striven for though not always achieved, to establish an independent judicial branch, neutral as between government and individual, class and class, party and party, and to utilize this independence and neutrality to maintain the principal balances upon which our system rests. The newer "democracy," however, denies that independence and neutrality can be a reality; but it also asserts that they are not even desirable in administering its system of law, which tolerates no judicial checks against dictatorship. I therefore propose to outline an appraisal of our supreme judicial establishment to determine the extent to which it may be relied upon to maintain the form of government we have established and prefer.

No sound assessment of our Supreme Court can treat it as an isolated, self-sustaining, or self-sufficient institution. It is a unit of a complex, interdependent scheme of government from which it cannot be severed. Nor can it be regarded merely as another law court. The Court's place in the combination was determined by principles drawn from a philosophy broader than mere law.

Our foundations were quarried not only from the legal ideas but also from the political, social, philosophical, scientific, and theological learnings of the eighteenth century, "the silver age of the Renaissance." All these were dominated by a belief in "the laws of nature and of nature's God." Faith in a "higher law," which had achieved a venerable place in the history of ideas through the speculations of jurists, monks, and scholars,[1] burst forth toward the end of the eighteenth century into a fanatical creed that took over French and American liberal thinking and led in each case to a violent revolution.[2]

Our judicial, executive, and legislative branches all were grounded in a belief that they were bound by the authority of a clear and universally acceptable natural law, revealed by man's reason and always and everywhere the same. Its fundamentals were proclaimed self-evident truths, as indisputable as the axioms of geometry, which needed only to be declared to be acknowledged as right and just by the opinion of mankind. These truths of natural law to that age stood as the ultimate sanction of liberty and justice, equality and toleration. The whole constitutional philosophy of the time was based on a system of values in which the highest was the freedom of the individual from interference by officialdom—the rights of man. To supplement this natural order, little man-made government was thought to be needed, and the less the better.

To make certain that these natural rights should have some man-made sanctions, the forefathers added ten Amendments to the original instrument, translating their version of the rights of man into legal limitations on the new government. They did not stop, as the French did, at reciting these in a preamble to the Constitution, where they served as an admonition only to a parliament that was all-powerful because there could be no judicial review of its legislation.[3] On the contrary, the forefathers established a Bill of Rights which conferred as a matter of law, enforceable in court, certain immunities and rights upon citizens which correspondingly limited the power of the majority duly expressed through governmental action. The whole spirit of this was to make secure the liberties which were what men in that age most wanted of the law. I find little indication that they foresaw a technique by which those liberties might be used to destroy themselves by immunizing a movement of a minority to impose upon the country an incompatible scheme of values which did not include political and civil liberties.[4] The resort to that technique in this country, however fruitless, contemporaneously with the collapse or capture of free governments abroad, has stirred American anxieties deeply.

What we face today on an intellectual level is the climax of a long-gathering conflict between opposite poles of thought. Our traditional high valuation of individual liberty conflicts with the totalitarians' higher valuation of group interest within the state. Communism, Naziism, and Fascism have each made phenomenally successful drives to capture the minds and loyalties of numerous and aspiring peoples for this philosophy so antithetic to our own.

It is not possible to detail all of the American trends which, rightly or wrongly, have cooled the zeal of our own people for the principles on which our government was founded. Our own indifference, deviations, and dissatisfactions are largely the reason why our principles make so anemic and sterile an appearance in the world-wide struggle for the minds of men. The majestic phrases of the forefathers, even as they were penned, were being drained of their fervor. Men were already ceasing to ask "What must I do to be saved?" and were asking "What can I do to become rich, powerful, and honored?"

As men's minds turned more to material advancement, and the industrial revolution introduced new means both to satisfy and to stimulate the acquisitive instincts, a riotous competition was touched off for the spoils of the world and for exploitation of working and consuming masses. The inherently obscure and oracular character of natural law led courts to respond to the pressure of the times by making it a sanction for *laissez faire;* and skeptics, historians, and jurists joined in discrediting it. The nineteenth century closed with Americans repeating the phrases of the Declaration of Independence about the laws of nature and of nature's God, but the real attitude was that attributed by Knickerbocker to the Connecticut Yankees, who resolved to be governed by the laws of God—until they found time to make better ones. The so-called positivists took over, and any command that some authority had physical power to enforce became law. Since the Nürnberg postmortem on the Hitler regime, few will believe that these positivist doctrines are weapons in the struggle to preserve liberty.[5]

Meanwhile, Marx and Engels, two strangers to the actual workings of our American system, had formulated the revolutionary scheme of values which under new leadership is now our world-wide rival. Their doctrine teaches that there is no such thing as natural law or impartial justice, that the law is and should be the weapon of the class in power and administered in its interests, that law rests on the authority of force and not on any inherent rightfulness, that the object of its protection is the dominant group rather than the individual, and that it should not be administered by neutral judges but by class-conscious and class-serving judges. The Communists reject our claims to liberty as abstract intellectualism, if not hypocrisy, and claim that our free government is a sham to conceal economic exploitation of the most numerous class—the proletariat—which should be aroused to support the Communists in containment of our system and its eventual overthrow.

Our forefathers' conception of a liberal legal order had been the dynamic ideology of most of the nineteenth century. But the twentieth century has seen the depressed masses in nearly all backward countries abandon it as their hope and turn to a militant Communism radiating from the Soviet Union, which Clement Attlee once described as merely "an inverted czardom." It dawns upon us that we are in an age of almost world-wide reaction, indeed, of counterrevolution, against the teachings and philosophy of our American Revolution and our Constitution. Revolutions in our time, whether by Communists, Fascists, or Nazis, have not pretended to overthrow or moderate the power of the state over the individual, but, instead, have each aspired to concentrate in the state a more absolute power over every activity of life and leave nothing but tatters of the "rights of man." Paradoxical as it may seem, we are in an age of rebellion against liberty.[6] The rise of this new doctrine has brought about one of the most bloody and cruel half-centuries in the annals of mankind, one which has put to death or enslaved more people solely because of racial or national origin and political or economic views or status than ever before in history. This violence that civilization has experienced was not a repetition of physical overthrow from barbarians without. Civilization is still threatened by forces generated within and perhaps by itself.

Fortunately, up to now America has escaped any catastrophic impact from this turn of events. With few exceptions these revolutionary ideas have made their appeal to those we have long deemed backward peoples. The old and the new did not confront each other in our country with such provocative contrasts as in some other lands. We entered each of the great wars late, and while our collective resources were strained, they were not exhausted. Individual living standards were depressed, but not to the point of misery. It is true that we have suffered some intellectual demoralization, which has proceeded far—to the point where speculative freedom is regarded as the equivalent of revolutionary action. But intolerance, suspicion, and hatred still resort only to verbal and legalistic weapons and have not sunk to a regime of physical violence.

Nevertheless, it would have been too much to expect that the American mind would be wholly free from the influence of counterrevolutionary currents of thought which have captivated other peoples or that each of the ideologies which have divided the rest of the world would not find some followers and sympathizers here. Unfortunately, liberal-minded citizens have sometimes become entangled with Communist teachings, while many conservative citizens have reacted by favoring some form of "strong" government controlled by themselves—the reaction which elsewhere brought about Naziism and Fascism. It is time that we reëxamine the strength and defects of our own system, for we cannot longer regard the world-wide revolt against its animating principles as a local or passing flash in the pan. The fact is that we face a rival, secularized system of faith and order spread with a religious fervor not witnessed since the tides of Islamic fanaticism receded. We are brought into sudden and bitter competition with a whole new concept of the nature and use of social and political organization, a rivalry for which we are prepared intellectually even less than militarily.

Against this background a study of the Supreme Court can hardly fail to be instructive. First, the Court is distinctively a product of our founders' philosophy in some of its most important functions, and no counterpart has existed or can exist in those areas of the world which have traded individual liberty for totalitarianism. Second, this Court, structurally and functionally, has survived an attempt by President Roosevelt to reorganize it so as to eliminate a "judicial activism" which was impairing a program supported by large popular majorities. Third, soon thereafter the Court passed, by the process of mortality and replacement, almost entirely into the hands of those who were its former critics, and they have now had over a decade of its control. Fourth, not one of the basic power conflicts which precipitated the Roosevelt struggle against the judiciary has been eliminated or settled, and the old conflict between the branches of the Government remains, ready to break out again whenever the provocation becomes sufficient.

We ought first to inquire what kind of institution the Supreme Court really is, the degree of its independence, the nature of its power, and the limitations on its capacity and effectiveness. In the second lecture we will consider it as a conventional law court administering the usual civil and criminal justice. Lastly, we will consider the Court as a political institution arbitrating the allocation of powers between different branches of the Federal Government, between state and nation, between state and state, and between majority government and minority rights.

The Supreme Court of the United States was created in a different manner from most high courts. In Europe, most judiciaries evolved as subordinates to the King, who delegated to them some of his functions. For example, while the English judges have developed a remarkably independent status, they still retain the formal status of Crown servants. But here, the Supreme Court and the other branches of the Federal Government came into existence at the same time and by the same act of creation. "We the People of the United States" deemed an independent Court equally as essential as a Congress or an Executive, especially, I suppose, to "establish Justice, insure domestic Tranquility," and to "secure the Blessings of Liberty to ourselves and to our Posterity." The status of the Court as a unit of the Government, not as an institution subordinate to it, no doubt has given it prestige, for the people do not regard the Justices as employees of the Government of the day or as civil servants, as in continental Europe. Also, federal judges enjoy two bulwarks of independence—life tenure (except for impeachable misbehavior) and irreducible salaries (except by taxation and inflation).

Nonetheless, the Constitution-makers left the Court in vital respects a dependent body. The political branches nominate and confirm the Justices, a control of the Court's composition which results in a somewhat lagging political influence over its trend of decision, and any party that prevails in the Federal Government through several presidential terms will gradually tend to impress its political philosophy on the Court. The political branches also from time to time may alter the number of Justices, and that power was used to influence the course of decision several times before it was again proposed by President Roosevelt.[7]

The Court also is dependent on the political branches for its powers in other vital respects. Its only irrevocable jurisdiction is original, and that reaches only cases affecting Ambassadors, public Ministers, or Consuls, or cases in which a state is a party. In all other cases it has appellate jurisdiction, but "with such exceptions and under such regulations as Congress shall make." One Congress, fearing a decision unfavorable to its post-Civil War enactments, ousted the court of jurisdiction in a case that had already been argued, and the Court submitted.[8] The Court also is dependent upon the political branches for the execution of its mandates, for it has no physical force at its command. The story is traditional that President Jackson once withheld enforcement, saying, "John Marshall has made his decision:— *now let him enforce it!*"[9] Also, the Court, of course, depends upon Congress for the appropriation of funds with which to operate. These all add up to a fairly formidable political power over the Supreme Court, if there were a disposition to exert it.

But perhaps the most significant and least comprehended limitation upon the judicial power is that this power extends only to cases and controversies. We know that this restriction was deliberate, for it was proposed in the Convention that the Supreme Court be made part of a Council of Revision with a kind of veto power, and this was rejected.[10]

The result of the limitation is that the Court's only power is to decide lawsuits between adversary litigants

with real interests at stake, and its only method of proceeding is by the conventional judicial, as distinguished
from legislative or administrative, process. This precludes the rendering of advisory opinions even at the re-
quest of the nation's President[11] and every form of pronouncement on abstract, contingent, or hypothetical issues.[12] It prevents acceptance for judicial settlement of
issues in which the interests and questions involved are
political in character.[13] It also precludes imposition on
federal constitutional courts of nonjudicial duties. Recent trends to empower judges to grant or deny wire-
tapping rights to a prosecutor or to approve a waiver
of prosecution in order to force a witness to give self-
incriminating testimony raise interesting and dubious
questions. A federal court can perform but one function
—that of deciding litigations—and can proceed in no
manner except by the judicial process.

In his pioneering studies, Judge Cardozo demonstrated that this is not the rigid and inflexible process
some of our ancestors thought it to be.[14] But its inherent
methods make it unfit for solving some kinds of problems which elements of our society have from time to
time expected the Supreme Court to settle.

While the President or the Congress can take up any
subject at any time, a court in our Anglo-American
system is a substantially passive instrument, to be moved
only by the initiative of litigants. The Supreme Court
cannot take most cases until at least one and generally
two courts below have heard and decided them, which,

with the present congestion of calendars, may be very long indeed. Also, as an appellate court, it properly can act only on the state of facts revealed by the record made in the court below,[15] supplemented sometimes by general information of which it may take judicial notice.[16] Hence a claim of right may be prejudiced by the incompetence, carelessness, or collusion of attorneys, as where they fail to make an adequate record to support the question sought to be raised. The decision of a case also may depend on its peculiarities of fact, for it is still true that hard cases make bad law. And when it is all over, the judicial decree, however broadly worded, actually binds, in most instances, only the parties to the case. As to others, it is merely a weather vane showing which way the judicial wind is blowing—a precedent that the Court in a similar case is likely to follow. Its real weight in subsequent cases, however, will depend on many factors, such as the quality of the prevailing opinion, the strength of any dissent, the acceptance or criticism by the profession, and the experience in application of the rule. Thus, the process of the courts is adapted to the intensive examination of particular legal grievances.

No conclusion as to what can be expected of the Court is valid which overlooks the measure of its incapacity to entertain and decide cases under its traditional working methods. With few exceptions, Congress has found it necessary to make review in the Supreme Court not the right of a litigant but a discretionary matter with the Court itself, in order to keep the volume of its business within its capacity. Last term, review was sought by appeal and certiorari in 1,452 cases, only 119 of which were allowed. It is not necessary to detail the considerations which move the Court to grant review beyond saying that the grant is not intended merely to give a litigant another chance, nor does it depend on the dollars involved or the private interests affected, but upon the importance of the case to a uniform and just system of federal law.

The routine during the Court term has been to hear arguments the first five days of each two weeks, followed by two weeks of recess for the writing of opinions and the study of the appeals and certiorari petitions, which must be disposed of periodically. The time allowed for each side to argue its case is normally one hour, and, in cases where the question seems not complex, it is half of that. In the early days of the Supreme Court, the volume of work permitted argument to extend over several days, as it still does in the House of Lords. Many cases argued before us today in two hours have taken days, weeks, and even months in the trial court or administrative body.

What really matters to the lawyer and the law is what happens between the argument and the decision. On each Saturday following argument or preceding a decision Monday, the Court holds its only regularly scheduled conference. It begins at 11 a.m. and rarely ends before 5:30 p.m. With a half-hour for lunch, this gives about 360 minutes in which to complete final consideration of forthcoming opinions, the noting of probable jurisdiction of appeals, the disposition of petitions for certiorari, petitions for rehearing and miscellaneous matters, and the decision of argued cases. The largest conference list during the October 1953 term contained 145 items, the shortest 24, the average 70. A little computation will show that the average list would permit, at the average conference, an average of five minutes of deliberation per item, or about 33 seconds of discussion per item by each of the nine Justices, assuming, of course, that each is an average Justice who does the average amount of talking.

All that saves the Court from being hopelessly bogged down is that many of these items are so frivolous on mere inspection that no one finds them worthy of discussion, and they are disposed of by unanimous consent. Even eliminating these, the time devoted at conference to argued cases is inadequate for detailed deliberation and results, more or less, in a canvass of impressions with the understanding that a vote on any case is tentative and on later consideration may be changed. And not infrequently the detailed study required to write an opinion, or the persuasiveness of an opinion or dissent, will lead to a change of a vote or even to a change of result. If there is further conferring, it is unofficial, usually between two or more Justices of like mind in the particular case.

The pressure of time may induce an attitude that

discussion in conference is futile and thereby contrib-
utes to the multiplicity of individual opinions. It is
often easier to write out one's own view than for nine
men in such short time to explore their doubts and
difficulties together, or to reach a reconciliation of view-
points. The fact is that the Court functions less as one
deliberative body than as nine, each Justice working
largely in isolation except as he chooses to seek consulta-
tion with others. These working methods tend to culti-
vate a highly individualistic rather than a group viewpoint.

The individual study which any case receives before
or after argument is the affair of each Justice. All receive
the printed briefs and record, in some cases short, in
others running to a great many volumes. Some records
take five feet of shelf space. It is easily demonstrated that
no Justice possibly could read more than a fraction of
the printed matter filed with the Court each year. Nor
is it necessary that he should. But as to his individual
labors, with this mountain of papers, each Justice is the
keeper of his own conscience.

In argued cases, conferences are followed by the prep-
aration and circulation of opinions by Justices desig-
nated by the Chief Justice when he is with the prevailing view and, if not, by the senior Associate who is. But
any Justice is free to write as he will, and there may be
one or more opinions concurring in the result but
reaching it by different reasons, and there may be a dissenting opinion or opinions. This occasions complaint

by laymen and the bar that they are required to piece all these contributions together in order to make out where the Supreme Court really stands as an institution.

All of this is at odds with the practice of most courts of continental Europe, which make it a rule to announce the decision in one statement only and to issue no dissents or concurrences. Moreover, their work is institutionalized and depersonalized. The court's opinion bears the name of no author. Like our *per curiam* opinion, it may be the work of any member or of several in collaboration. This anonymity diminishes any temptation to exploit differences within the court, but it may also diminish the incentive for hard work on opinions. In any event, I am sure that not only Anglo-American tradition but judicial and professional opinion favors the identification of writers and the full disclosure of important differences within the Court. Mr. Jefferson would have required each Justice to write his reasons in every case, as proof that he gave it consideration and did not merely follow a leader.[17]

The dissenting opinion strives to undermine the Court's reasoning and discredit its result. At its best, the dissent, as Mr. Hughes said, is "an appeal to the brooding spirit of the law, to the intelligence of a future day. . . ."[18] But Judge Cardozo has written:

". . . Comparatively speaking at least, the dissenter is irresponsible. The spokesman of the court is cautious, timid, fearful of the vivid word, the heightened phrase.

He dreams of an unworthy brood of scions, the spawn of careless *dicta,* disowned by the *ratio decidendi,* to which all legitimate offspring must be able to trace their lineage. The result is to cramp and paralyze. One fears to say anything when the peril of misunderstanding puts a warning finger to the lips. Not so, however, the dissenter. . . . For the moment, he is the gladiator making a last stand against the lions. The poor man must be forgiven a freedom of expression, tinged at rare moments with a touch of bitterness, which magnanimity as well as caution would reject for one triumphant."[19]

Dissent has a popular appeal, for it is an underdog judge pleading for an underdog litigant. Of course, one party or the other must always be underdog in a lawsuit, the purpose of which really is to determine which one it shall be. But the tradition of great dissents built around such names as Holmes, Brandeis, Cardozo, and Stone is not due to the frequency or multiplicity of their dissents, but to their quality and the importance of the few cases in which they carried their disagreement beyond the conference table. Also, quite contrary to the popular notion, relatively few of all the dissents recorded in the Supreme Court have later become law, although some of these are of great importance.

There has been much undiscriminating eulogy of dissenting opinions. It is said they clarify the issues. Often they do the exact opposite. The technique of the dissenter often is to exaggerate the holding of the Court beyond the meaning of the majority and then to blast away at the excess. So the poor lawyer with a similar case does not know whether the majority opinion meant what it seemed to say or what the minority said it meant. Then, too, dissenters frequently force the majority to take positions more extreme than was originally intended. The classic example is the *Dred Scott Case*,[20] in which Chief Justice Taney's extreme statements were absent in his original draft and were inserted only after Mr. Justice McLean, then a more than passive candidate for the presidency, raised the issue in dissent.

The *right of dissent* is a valuable one. Wisely used on well-chosen occasions, it has been of great service to the profession and to the law. But there is nothing good, for either the Court or the dissenter, in dissenting per se. Each dissenting opinion is a confession of failure to convince the writer's colleagues, and the true test of a judge is his influence in leading, not in opposing, his court.

If the Supreme Court were any kind of institution except a court, it would be easy to suggest methods by which it could dispose of an increased volume of work. The objection to most such proposals is that they are incompatible with the personal and individual responsibility inherent in judicial office.

It has been suggested that a small committee of the Court could pass on certiorari applications. Some lawyers believe that this is done. That is not true. The Supreme Court does not function on any case by com-

mittee. Every qualified Justice acts on every petition expressly or by acquiescence.

It is often suggested that the Court could create a staff
of assistants like those of administrative tribunals to
take much of the drudgery of judicial work from the
Justices. In fact, a suspicion has grown at the bar that the
law clerks already constitute a kind of junior court
which decides the fate of certiorari petitions. This idea
of the law clerks' influence gave rise to a lawyer's wag-
gish statement that the Senate no longer need bother
about confirmation of Justices but ought to confirm the
appointment of law clerks. Twice during the last term
I was asked by prominent lawyers, once by letter and
once orally, how they could get their petitions for certiorari past law clerks and to the consideration of the Justices themselves. The answer is that every petition is on
the conference list, and its fate is decided by the vote or
agreement without formal vote of every Justice who
does not disqualify himself.

The extent and methods of utilizing law clerks' serv-
ices naturally differ with the individual Justices. The
law clerks regard themselves and are regarded not as
aides to the Court, but as aides to the particular Justice
who selects them. What a Justice delegates to his clerk
will depend on the Justice's temperament and experience, but it is he who is responsible for his contribution
to the Court's work. For myself, I believe that a court is
one place where counsel should confront and address
the very men who are to decide his case. I do not think

judging can be a staff job, and I deplore whatever tendency there may be in the courts to make it such.

There have been suggestions that an increased work
capacity could be obtained by enlarging the Court,
which might then sit in sections or chambers[21] as do
some administrative bodies in this country and many
courts abroad. The French Cour de Cassation and the
Soviet Supreme Court both consist of sixty to seventy
members who function, in fact, as several courts, each
dealing with a specialized type of litigation; as, for
example, commercial cases, other civil cases, criminal
cases, military appeals, cases involving officials of the
government, and admiralty cases. But our Constitution
vests the judicial power in only "one supreme Court,"
and it has been the view of high authority that this precludes the Court from being split into chambers or sections; also, there has never been either political or professional sentiment in this country in favor of such a
Supreme Court, and it would face very practical difficulties even if it were permissible under the Constitution.[22]

The only way found practicable or acceptable in this
country for keeping the volume of cases within the
capacity of a court of last resort is to allow the inter-
mediate courts of appeal finally to settle all cases that
are of consequence only to parties. This reserves to the
court of last resort only questions on which lower courts
are in conflict or those of general importance to the law.

From what I have said it might almost be assumed

that the Supreme Court could be ignored in the power equation of the American Government. But in living history this institution has profoundly influenced, for better or for worse, the course of the nation. Not only has it been the center of bitter debate itself, but its decisions have played some part in nearly every great political issue that has vexed our people.

What authority does the Court possess which generates this influence? The answer is its power to hold unconstitutional and judicially unenforceable an act of the President, of Congress, or of a constituent state of the Federation. That power is not expressly granted or hinted at in the Article defining judicial power, but rests on logical implication. It is an incident of jurisdiction to determine what really is the law governing a particular case or controversy. In the hierarchy of legal values, if the higher law of the Constitution prohibits what the lower law of the legislature attempts, the latter is a nullity; otherwise, the Constitution would exist only at the option of Congress. Thus it comes about that in a private litigation the Court may decide a question of power that will be of great moment to the nation or to a state.

The assertion of this power over the enactments of the states met with strong resistance, and its application to laws of Congress provoked bitter and persistent opposition. It is needless to trace the evolution of the power as now exercised. The Rooseveltian struggle with the Court did not impair the power, which is as positively

asserted today as in pre-Roosevelt days. But neither did
that struggle end the controversy over the proper use
of the power, a controversy which lies just beneath the
surface and is likely to break forth from time to time as
long as the Republic shall last.

Public opinion, however, seems always to sustain the
power of the Court, even against attack by popular executives and even though the public more than once has
repudiated particular decisions. It is inescapable in our
form of government that authority exist somewhere to
interpret an instrument which sets up our whole structure and defines the powers of the Federal Government
in about 4,000 words, to which a century and a half
have added only about half as many amendatory words.
The people have seemed to feel that the Supreme Court,
whatever its defects, is still the most detached, dispas-
sionate, and trustworthy custodian that our system af-
fords for the translation of abstract into concrete constitutional commands.

The Constitution has gone through several cycles of
interpretation, each of which is related to the political
and economic condition of the period. Federal powers
were consolidated and invigorated under Marshall. A
reaction marked by conflict over the very nature and
binding force of the compact embittered the time of
Taney. There followed a period when attention turned
to nationalism and to railroad building and industrial
growth stimulated by a long period of almost uninter-
rupted peace. That came to an end in 1914, and we

entered the period of international violence which now
burdens and vexes us and puts our internal liberties
under new strains.

That the Supreme Court, in some instances, can in-
terpose judicial authority between political forces and
those whose liberty they would override is a great dis-
tinction from those governments abroad which have
been subverted by dictatorship. But I have tried to
point out that while our judiciary is an effective instrument for applying to the case of an individual the just
laws enacted by representatives of a freedom-respecting
society, it has grave jurisdictional, procedural, and political shortcomings. These counsel against leaving the
protection of liberty wholly to the judiciary, while heed-
lessly allowing the elected branches of the Government
to be constituted without regard to their members' attitudes toward liberty.

Let us take the factor of delay. Since the Court may
pronounce a judgment of unconstitutionality only in
deciding a case or controversy, obviously it cannot take
the initiative in checking what the Justices may know to
be constitutional violations. It has no self-starting capacity and must await the action of some litigant so ag-
grieved as to have a justiciable case. Also, its pronouncement must await the decision in the lower courts. Often
it is years after a statute is put on the books and begins
to take effect before a decision on a constitutional question can be heard by the Supreme Court. The Smith Act
of 1940 was held constitutional for the first time in

1951,[23] and the Alien Registration Act, also of 1940, was passed on in 1952.[24] The run of constitutional litigation, like that of all litigations, is slow and costly.

Such delays often mean that the damage is done before the remedy for invasion of civil liberties is available. For example: In 1951 the Court cast serious doubt upon the legality of the Attorney General's list of subversive organizations promulgated in 1947.[25] But the list had long been widely circulated and accepted, and despite the Court's views it has never ceased to be used in the press, in the executive department, by and before congressional committees, and even in courts to prejudice individuals in their liberty, position, and good name.

Then, too, many of the most vital acts of government cannot be challenged at all by the case and controversy route, because the questions are political or involve the spending power,[26] foreign affairs,[27] or the war power.[28] The Supreme Court is a tribunal of limited jurisdiction, narrow processes, and small capacity for handling mass litigation; it has no force to coerce obedience, and is subject to being stripped of jurisdiction or smothered with additional Justices any time such a disposition exists and is supported strongly enough by public opinion. I think the Court can never quite escape consciousness of its own infirmities, a psychology which may explain its apparent yielding to expediency, especially during war time.[29]

If I may borrow a summation from my former self, I

will repeat to you the conclusion of a lecture to the lawyers of the Ministry of Justice of France, delivered at their invitation in April 1946, when they were in the throes of writing a new constitution for France. After discussing the judicial vis-à-vis the political power in our system, I said:

"Opinion, of course, will differ as to the advantages and disadvantages of this constitutional and judicial system. The United States on the whole has been a prosperous country, with varied resources, making a favorable background for any experiment in government. Its inhabitants have not faced the strains that beset some less-favored nations. Even so, our history has not been free of sanguinary internal conflicts. It would not be realistic to contend that judicial power always has been used wisely. The Court has been sharply attacked by Presidents Jefferson, Jackson, Lincoln, and both Roosevelts. Yet no substantial sentiment exists for any curtailment of the Court's powers. Even President Roosevelt in the bitterest conflict with judicial power in our history suggested only change in the Court's composition, none in its constitutional prerogatives. The real strength of the position of the Court is probably in its indispensability to government under a written Constitution. It is difficult to see how the provisions of a 150-year-old written document can have much vitality if there is not some permanent institution to translate them into current commands and to see to their contemporary application. Courts will differ from time to time in the em-

phasis they will place on one or another of the Constitution's provisions, in part no doubt responsive to the
atmosphere of the changes in public opinion. Interpretations will change from one generation to another,
precedents will sometimes be overruled, innovations
will be made that will not always be predictable. This
always has been the history of the Supreme Court.

"The legal profession in all countries knows that
there are only two real choices of government open to a
people. It may be governed by law or it may be governed by the will of one or of a group of men. Law, as the
expression of the ultimate will and wisdom of a people,
has so far proven the safest guardian of liberty yet devised. I think our constitutional and judicial system has
made a valuable and enduring contribution to the
science of government under law. We commend it to
your notice, not because we think it is perfect, but because it is an earnest effort to fulfill those aspirations for
freedom and the general welfare which are a common
heritage of your people and of mine."

II

THE SUPREME COURT

as a Law Court

THE position of the Supreme Court as chief judicial organ of the Government brings to its docket many kinds of cases. But here we will deal with only a few which illustrate its functions as a law court.

No one seems to have doubted the necessity for a federal judicial establishment at least to decide cases arising under the Federal Constitution, statutes, and treaties, and thus to maintain the supremacy of federal law in its proper field. But neither the text of the Constitution nor the debates in the Constitutional Convention gave any clear forecast of the part the Court was expected to play. If the forefathers thought in terms of the familiar, they thought of a court to hear litigations between John Doe and Richard Roe or criminal cases. They undoubtedly did not anticipate the kind of litigation that today constitutes most of the docket of the Supreme Court.

The Constitution and the Judiciary Act of 1789[30] so far as federal cases were concerned launched a Court without a jurisprudence, which is somewhat like launching a ship without a rudder. The Court of course had no tradition of its own; codification had not become the practice, and English law was no longer authority. We are likely to assume that adherence to the common law was inevitable and unopposed. That does not appear to be true in the conditions of that time. In the aftermath of the Revolution, British law was unpopular with the masses, and some states went so far as to prohibit lawyers from citing British precedents in arguments before state courts. The common law known to the literate population was the common law of Blackstone, who "described rather its theory than its practice, and its theory was many years behind its practice."[31] Lord Mansfield was still Chief Justice of the King's Bench, and his reforms had not settled into the legal thought of his time. Severe critics of the common law said it was feudal and aristocratic, rigid and subtle. Its most fanatical advocates had to admit that it would require radical adaptations to the American concept of government and justice.

The Supreme Court was not bound to any particular body of learning for guidance. When the Court moved to Washington in 1800, it was provided with no books, which probably accounts for the high quality of early opinions. In five of Marshall's great opinions he cited not a single precedent. The leading commentators, Kent and Story, frequently cited civil law authorities, chiefly from Dutch or French sources. But most lawyers turned to what was written in the language they knew, and the common law thus conditioned their thought and argument about the legal problems of the new country.

A very important part of the common law of England was its law of crimes. In our day of prolific legislation we are prone to think that there can be no crime unless a specific statute makes the act criminal. But acts harmful to the community were punished by judges as crimes long before there were legislatures—in fact, many crimes at common law are yet undefined by legislatures, and some states still have common law offenses. So federal judges, pursuant to common law practices, began to assert the power to indict and try for acts that they deemed offenses, although no statute so provided. This touched off a controversy.

Under the judges, English criminal law had become harsh to the point of savagery. There were at least 160 capital offenses in the reign of George III, including stealing one shilling from a pocket or stealing a sheep. Judge-made law also had the weakness revealed by William Penn in Old Bailey, when he asked, "By what Law it is you prosecute me?" and was told, "Upon the Common Law." When he persisted, "Where is that Common Law?" the Recorder, so 'tis said, replied, "You must not think that I am able to run up so many years, and over so many adjudged Cases, which we call Common Law, to answer your curiosity."[32] Americans, too, had some curiosity as to the law under which federal judges were assuming to try for crimes, and the Jeffersonian party was strongly opposed to this extension of judicial power.

In 1812 the Supreme Court put to rest the division of opinion which had theretofore prevailed and held that the courts of the United States have no common law criminal jurisdiction. Crimes against the United States must be made so by Congressional Act: *United States v. Hudson and Goodwin,* 7 Cranch (11 U.S.) 32, and *United States v. Coolidge,* 1 Wheat. (14 U.S.) 415. The opinions in these cases were written by Mr. Justice Johnson, Mr. Jefferson's first appointee to the Court. They cite no authority, but the *Hudson and Goodwin* opinion significantly observes that "although this question is brought up now for the first time to be decided by this Court, we consider it as having been long since settled in public opinion." Thus the Court, itself, anticipated by a century Mr. Dooley's remark that it follows the election returns. These early cases show how thin is the line that separates law and politics. The law they made has remained to this time.

These decisions did not settle the question of where

the Court was to find its law to govern disputes in federal civil cases. Statements such as that of Mr. Justice Brandeis in *Erie R. Co.* v. *Tompkins*,[33] "There is no federal general common law," are sometimes read as meaning that there is no federal common law, general or otherwise. That is not my understanding. In the beginning the Court sought light, and may yet seek light, from any body of learning, but it has built up, and still is building up, a body of federal common law. This is not general law, because most legal relationships are not federally governed, but it has all the characteristics of common law for federal purposes. On the same day that *Erie R. Co.* v. *Tompkins* was decided, Mr. Justice Brandeis wrote in another case that "whether the water of an interstate stream must be apportioned between the two States is a question of 'federal common law' upon which neither the statutes nor the decisions of either State can be conclusive."[34] The federal courts by the familiar judicial process are making a common law on federal questions, sometimes departing from the common law of the states because of the Federal Government's interest.[35] And so, had the federal courts been confined to cases involving federal questions, they would have proceeded with little that was unique or perplexing to those familiar with the nature of the judicial process.

But the Constitution, in addition to giving federal jurisdiction because of the nature of the question involved, created a federal jurisdiction based upon the

status of the litigants—that is, federal jurisdiction of
cases between citizens of different states—regardless of
what law is involved.

The Judiciary Act of 1789 infringed on the function
of state courts in two respects. It provided for a review
by the Supreme Court of final judgments of the highest
state courts in cases in which federal questions are involved, and it also established a system of federal trial
courts throughout the United States and vested them
with jurisdiction of controversies "by a citizen of the
state in which the suit is brought against a citizen of
another state."[36] The purpose of the latter provision
had no relation to the enforcement of federal law but
was to provide a federal forum, more neutral and free
from the influences of localism than the courts of a state
afforded to those not its citizens. It is difficult today to
judge whether in 1789 the fear that state courts might
do less than justice to out-of-state litigants was war-
ranted. Since the jurors for either federal or state courts
would be drawn from the same locality, they would
seem to carry the same prejudices into the jury box of
either court. The anticipated difference between the
federal courts and the local courts must have been in
the exercise of the judicial function. We must remember that following the Revolution many state courts
were manned by laymen, and state law and procedure
were frequently in an unsettled condition. The colonial
and state courts did not enjoy high prestige, and their
opinions were not even deemed worthy of publication.

There was but one small American law school, and only William and Mary had a full-time law professorship. James Wilson in Philadelphia and James Kent at Columbia each attempted a course of law lectures, but both were abandoned because of a lack of interest. The bookshelf of the American lawyer was barren of books on American law, or on any law from an American viewpoint. A survey of the hundred years ending in 1788 concluded that "not a single book that could be called a treatise intended for the use of professional lawyers was published in the British Colonies and the American States. All of the books within this period which by any stretch of definition might be regarded as legal treatises were for the use of laymen."[37]

There are so many imponderables involved that I yield to the judgment of men who lived at that time that local courts so little guided by law might have been a crude and hostile forum for the stranger. I may readily believe that diversity jurisdiction had justifications in the time of its creation without believing that it has justifications now.

The Act of 1789 commanded that the laws of the several states be regarded as rules of decision in trials at common law in courts of the United States in cases where they apply. This was a simple rule to apply if there chanced to be an applicable state statute, but in that day few subjects had been codified or reduced to statute. Did this command of the Congress require the federal courts to apply the decisional law of the state courts in addition to the statutory laws of the several states? *Swift* v. *Tyson,* 16 Pet. (41 U.S.) 1, decided that the federal courts were not bound by state decisions in matters of general common law as regards commercial transactions. The Supreme Court, like Lord Mansfield, whom it quoted, held that the law of the commercial world was entitled to govern such transactions instead of local decisions, which it thought were not "laws" within the Judiciary Act. And in other cases, if the federal judge was obliged to entertain a case but found no state statute and no state decisions on the issue, what was he to do? Even where there were state decisions in cases governed thereby, what if they were muddled and plainly out of line with the general tenor of well-considered decisions on the subject? Strong men like Story and Marshall were not easily bound to local mediocrity and did not hesitate to declare the law as they saw it. The result over the years was the growth of a federal common law, independent of state law; and in some fields, such as unfair competition, this was a much-needed law which if left to state courts could hardly have developed because of their limited territorial jurisdiction.

This dual system for application of state law was bound to produce conflicts, for if a litigant could get his case into federal court, it might be decided by a more favorable rule than that of the state court. There was much shopping for favorable forums, and no doubt there were serious abuses which led the Supreme Court to reconsider and overrule *Swift* v. *Tyson* in *Erie R. Co.* v. *Tompkins*, 304 U.S. 64. The Court said that experience with the old rule had "revealed its defects, political and social,"[38] and the Court in overruling it swung to the opposite extreme. It declared that except in matters governed by the Federal Constitution or by Acts of Congress, the law to be applied by the federal courts is the law of the state, and decisions of the highest state courts are a part of such law. It pronounced the severe judgment on itself that its former rule "invaded rights" "reserved by the Constitution to the several States."[39]

Erie R. Co. v. *Tompkins* did not end the confusion, the conflict or the shopping for forums. But I think it does end the last vestige of justification for continuing this system of dual jurisdictions based on diversity of citizenship. All the concern and bother about discrimination and advantage are beside the point. The whole purpose of diversity jurisdiction is to give one of the parties a better break in federal court than he would expect in state court. Take that away, use the same jurors, make the federal judge rule as a state judge would rule, and the purpose sought in diversity jurisdiction is gone.

Moreover, confusion and conflict are just as inevitable under *Erie R. Co.* v. *Tompkins* as before. Some cases are now decided by federal courts on the basis of a theoretical "state law" which really does not exist because there is no state decision in point.[40] Lower state court decisions are controlling the final result of litigations in federal court, whereas they might be overruled if they were rendered in the state system.[41] A litigant's chance to reach the Supreme Court on the question of whether state law is misapplied, though promised by the Court's rules,[42] is zero. And a flood of state litigation is being diverted into federal courts. More than half of the private civil litigation in federal courts today consists of diversity of citizenship cases, and many of these are brought or removed to federal court for the purpose of avoiding state court decisions, although only questions of state law are involved. This category of litigation increased almost 80 per cent between 1945 and 1950. These cases are the major cause of congestion in federal courts, preventing litigants with legitimate federal questions from obtaining early disposition of their federal cases. The problem of which court has jurisdiction and which state law is applicable and whether it has been applied exactly as a state court would have done, is perplexing to the point of frustration to any person who tries to solve the question in a particular case without the consolation of a retainer. A vast and utterly unjustifiable part of federal litigation concerns only the question of jurisdiction, on which great time and labor and expense are expended before the merits of a question are ever reached.

In my judgment the greatest contribution that Congress could make to the orderly administration of justice in the United States would be to abolish the jurisdiction of the federal courts which is based solely on the ground that the litigants are citizens of different states.

It recently has been contended that the Constitution contemplated that the Supreme Court would be an independent and supreme expounder of the general common law for all states of the Union and thus provide for the whole country a uniform system of common law which all state courts would be bound to apply. This is quite contrary to any position now or ever taken by the Court. I am unable to accept the view that the Supreme Court was intended to reduce all state courts to a subordinate position, nor do I think it at all clear that the interests of the country would be served or the interest of justice advanced by requiring a uniform common law in all the states of the Union. Certainly it would be beyond the capacity of the present Court or any single court to resolve all the conflicts between judicial decisions in the state courts on common law questions. It would be a task of appalling magnitude, as any one will see who is familiar with the work of the American Law Institute on Restatement of the Law on any subject. Nor is the Supreme Court particularly adapted to the solution of the common law questions which pertain to the great body of private law. The Court is, long has been, and is likely to be, made up largely of men of wider political experience than of legal experience in the types of problems that confront the state courts. These private law questions have come before the Supreme Court only rarely, and the Court cannot give the close and frequent consideration to matters of private civil law that the state courts of final resort have been accustomed to do.

While a few of our state tribunals have not been distinguished for ability, I cannot find that over the years the Supreme Court of the United States has given better account of itself than have the highest courts of several of the states of the Union.

If we consider two branches of private civil law which have undergone radical modification, it will appear that they would not have been better handled by the Supreme Court than by local courts.

The eastern states generally adopted, along with the law of England, the doctrine of riparian ownership, which included the right to have the waters of a stream flow in its natural channel, undiminished in quantity and quality. These states worked out many variations which allowed the private development of water-power sites, conditioned upon liability for injury to the riparian rights of others, and made various other adaptations of the common law rule. Most of the members of the Supreme Court of the United States always have come from areas in which this doctrine prevails. With the opening up of the arid states in the West and the conflict between the mining interests in the mountains and the farming interests in the valley, there gradually grew up a system of appropriative rights in water which in those regions, by local decisional law, supplanted the common law riparian rule. The whole West agrees that the appropriative system was best adapted to its region. Would not a common law system of which the Supreme Court was the sole arbiter have adhered to the old rule, and would a Court whose purpose was uniformity have adapted itself to the locality?[43] Indeed, how could one Supreme Court declare one uniform common law of flowing waters which preserved riparian rights in the East and appropriative rights in the West? Uniformity of general private law throughout a country as large as ours is not desirable and I can find no satisfactory evidence that it was intended.

Another example is the development of oil and gas law. Just before the Civil War large quantities of oil and gas were discovered in western Pennsylvania and New York. These vagrant minerals moved about many feet below ground. Were they subject to ownership; if so, when and by whom? There was no law upon the subject. In the country courthouses the local bar and judges drew on all the learning they had for analogies and precepts and worked out a law of oil and gas which was adapted to the peculiarities of an industry with which they were intimately familiar. I cannot believe that a Supreme Court, most of whose members would have been strangers to the whole subject matter, would have done better.

As matters stand in the field of private civil law, aside from deciding questions of federal law, the Supreme Court seems to have no function except to see that lower federal courts do not resort to their independent judgment of a state's common law. If the lower courts guess at it, however wrongly, there is no instance where they have been reversed. If they think it out independently, they may be rebuked. The Supreme Court is exerting no influence today in the direction of uniformity even on subjects on which, as evidenced by the wide adoption of uniform statutes on commercial law, uniformity is desirable. There seems to be no further logical reason for federal courts to decide state lawsuits.

But there is one respect in which federal law is a powerful auxiliary to state law and to state court judgments. Only by virtue of federal law can they be made effective beyond the borders of the enacting or rendering state, which in many cases is where, if anywhere, they will have practical effect.

The Constitution sets forth a delusively simple requirement that "full faith and credit shall be given in each state to the public acts, records, and judicial proceedings of every other state. And the Congress may by general laws prescribe the manner in which such acts, records and proceedings shall be proved and the effect thereof." The first Congress, in 1790, prescribed the manner of authenticating legislative acts and proving judicial proceedings, and declared that they "shall have such faith and credit given to them in every court within the United States, as they have by law or usage in the courts of the state from whence the said records are or shall be taken."[44]

The principal use of these provisions has been to require recognition of a judgment of a state court outside of the rendering state. But the Supreme Court has laid down certain conditions, the most important and

frequently invoked of which is that the jurisdiction of
the court rendering a judgment is open to inquiry by
the court asked to enforce it. The principle seems logical enough in requiring that before a judgment is en-
forced it be found to be genuine and valid. The difficulty
is that jurisdiction turns on the facts, the facts are often
in dispute, and one court believing one set of witnesses
may infer one conclusion while a second court believing
the other group may infer the opposite.

Such issues have arisen chiefly in cases of divorce and
of multiple taxation. In both classes of cases the issue
as to jurisdiction usually turns on findings of domicile.
The Court has held that findings by the enforcing state
contrary to those of the rendering state are permissible.
This causes some strange results. A woman who is validly
a man's wife in the state where they live may not be his
widow in another; one who is no longer his wife may
become his widow.[45] An estate may owe death duties
to several states because each claims the deceased as a
domiciliary, and the Supreme Court will not interfere[46]
unless the aggregate demands are more than the estate,
at which point it will determine which state must lose
by the deficit.[47]

As to the extraterritorial effect of statutes, the cases
have been concerned chiefly with laws regulating corporations[48] and those setting up systems of workmen's
compensation.[49] Laws of both types sometimes have been
held to follow their subjects into another state and control rights and liabilities there. There has not been ex-

tensive resort to the Supreme Court to determine the faith and credit due to statutory or decisional law, perhaps because the state courts themselves have shown considerable respect for the laws of sister states.

The Court has held that, where the question is which law of two or more states is applicable, the rule as to conflict of laws of the state in which the suit is brought is conclusive, and the conflict does not present a federal question.[50] I find this doctrine difficult to reconcile with the purposes of the Full Faith and Credit Clause, which requires credit for public acts as well as judicial judgments. The forum of a suit may be determined fortuitously by where a defendant can be found for service, or it may be chosen purposely for some advantage found in its law. To allow choice of law to be made in effect by one of the parties or by fortuitous circumstances is not consistent with a rational system of justice.[51]

In a federal system, a person, an event, or a controversy must have some fixed place in law. Local policies and the balance of local interests, the avoidance of process by a defendant, or the shopping for a favorable forum by a plaintiff should not introduce disorder into our system. It seems to me that disagreement as to which of conflicting or competing state laws applies raises a federal question under the Full Faith and Credit Clause and that our hope for a better general legal system would be well served by wider application of that clause. It cannot be doubted that the power of Congress under the clause could resolve many tangles, especially in di-

vorce, alimony, and custody cases. Bills have been introduced to do so. The Court has repeatedly suggested congressional action, but inertia is one of the strongest
forces in both law and politics.

One of the fields of contest in which private right has
been posed against public authority lies in the orders of
administrative commissions and bodies. The rise of these
administrative agencies to become a virtual fourth
branch of the Government was not foreseen by the Con-
stitution-builders, and the relations of these agencies to
the three established branches have long perplexed the
courts. As the nation became so vast and life so complex
and interdependent as to require governmental regulation of some activities, experience revealed certain inherent limitations in all three original branches which
creation of the administrative body was expected to over-
come. Congress was inexpert and hurried and unable to
anticipate detailed problems of regulation and provide
positive or complete rules for their solution. A purely
executive agency could not be depended upon to apply
enactments of broad generalities without partisan or
prosecutive zeal. The courts were bound by the judicial
process, which was too slow and rigid to handle mass
problems of regulation. Hence, a century after the Constitution, the first federal commission made its appearance, and in recent years such bodies have multiplied
rapidly. They combine delegated rule-making, the investigation and prosecution of complaints, and adjudication, and are supposed to unite congressional judgment

as to policy, executive efficiency in enforcement, and
judicial neutrality and detachment of decision.

From the outset there has been great controversy as
to the place of these commissions in our constitutional
system. Lawyers by habit and training resisted their en-
croachment on the adjudicative function. A lawyer pre-
fers to be before a judge who does nothing but judge,
who has no responsibility for initiating the proceedings
or for the collection of evidence or the policy of the case.
He does not like a tribunal whose staff takes part in the
starting, conducting, and deciding of the case. The lawyer's opposition has been strengthened by his client's
frequent dislike of the regulatory legislation being en-
forced. The regulatory commission is the very heart of
such social and economic legislation, and if the heart
fails the whole body perishes. So some of the striking
at the commissions has really been striking at the reforms.

Nevertheless, there is much truth in the report rendered during the Roosevelt administration that government commissions were "in reality miniature independent governments set up to deal with the railroad problem, the banking problem, or the radio problem. They
constitute a headless 'fourth branch' of the Government,
a haphazard deposit of irresponsible agencies and un-
coordinated powers."[52] In forwarding that report to
Congress, President Roosevelt apparently agreed that
"the practice of creating independent regulatory commissions, who perform administrative work in addition

to judicial work, threatens to develop a 'fourth' branch of the Government, for which there is no sanction in the Constitution."[53] Yet he created more than any prior administration, and in vetoing the Walter-Logan bill to regulate their procedure with great strictness he expressed a more favorable estimate of their necessity and usefulness.[54]

It is too late in the day to continue the argument as to whether these statutory bodies which defy the constitutional principle of separation of powers are unconstitutional. They have been accepted as a valid part of our legal system.[55] But for three quarters of a century Congress has continued to launch these agencies without facing and resolving the administrative law problems which their functions precipitated.

The painfully logical French went about the controlling of official action where it affected the rights of the citizen in exactly the opposite manner. They recognized from the beginning that controversies between the citizen and an official, in the performance of his duty as he saw it, involved some different elements and considerations than the contest between two private citizens over private matters. They invested the Conseil d'Etat with jurisdiction over regulatory bodies and recognized that *droit administratif* was a different matter than private law, as to which the Cour de Cassation was the high court.[56]

But the United States and England have backed into the whole problem rather than face it. We treated the

controversy with the official as a matter of *ultra vires*—
if he was outside of his authority he was unofficial and
just another citizen. Thus, originally a suit for the return
of illegally exacted taxes was a private suit against the
one who collected the tax. If it was an illegal tax, he
was not acting as collector but as an unauthorized ex-
tortioner. Of course, we have had to abandon that ap-
proach and set up a system of refunds against the Government, but the earlier method of thinking has colored
our whole development of administrative law.

The courts have at three points in the administrative
process exerted a supervisory power. First: The administrative body can issue, but cannot by contempt proceedings enforce, its subpoena. If the witness is recal-
citrant, the power of the court is invoked. Just how far
the court should inquire into the propriety of issuing
as well as the power to issue the subpoena has been a
subject of much litigation. The courts have wavered
between strong protection for the right of privacy and
strong support for the right of public inquiry.[57] Second:
Decisions of these bodies with a few exceptions are subject to some measure of direct court review. Third:
These tribunals cannot use the contempt power to enforce their decrees and must seek enforcement orders
from the courts, at which point the legality of the decree
is open to challenge.

The measure of finality which should, or constitution-
ally can, be accorded to the administrative decision has
perhaps been the greatest source of litigation. The pow-

ers contended for have ranged from the most unbridled and unreviewable power to the most rigidly reviewable. Perhaps the most extreme argument was made under the Presidency of Taft and the Attorney Generalship of Wickersham in *Interstate Commerce Comm'n* v. *Louisville & Nashville R. Co.,* 227 U.S. 88, when the Government contended that findings by the Commission were binding on the Court even though there was no evidence in the record to sustain them and no opportunity was given the adverse party to test, explain, or refute them. The theory was that the Court must presume the Commission had adequate evidence even if not put in the record, a position which was rejected. The case illustrates the groping for law in this field in 1912. But the courts recognized that mingled with a judicial function were executive and legislative ones. On the one hand they tried to avoid supervising intermingled nonjudicial functions, on the other to prevent arbitrary invasion of private rights. The limit of review wavered from case to case, the courts being on the whole more restrictive of their own jurisdiction than Congress desired. Finally an Administrative Procedure Act was passed to effect some separation of prosecutive and adjudicative functions, to provide better and more independent hearing officers, and to enlarge the scope of judicial review. So far as administrative decisions are concerned, it would seem that if this headless fourth branch has a head, it must be the Supreme Court.

But judicial control is not the only kind of control

to which these bodies might be subject. They are dependent for annual appropriations on Congress, which
appropriately can inquire whether its policies are being
carried out according to its interest. The Taft-Hartley
Act did make a beginning at some such supervision of
the National Labor Relations Board. Then, too, there is
the potent influence of the Executive in making appointments, since the terms of commissioners are frequently
short. But the Supreme Court has refused to allow the
President to augment his influence through appointment
by adding the influence of removal for difference in
policy.[58]

The influence of the courts on administrative law is
steady and consistent as compared with the influence of
the President, which is really evident only with the ad-
vent of an administration with a new philosophy. That
has become evident in the past two years, when several
commissions by change of personnel have come to take
a very different view of their powers and of the ends for
which their powers should be used.

It is not difficult to sustain the right of a commission
within its delegated powers to change its policy pro-
spectively from time to time. The right of self-correction
is not an exclusive prerogative of the judiciary. But different questions arise when the change is retroactive,
especially when the commission or the court has already
issued its decrees enforcing the policy later abandoned.
This practice is pointed up by the recent case of *Rosen-
blum* v. *Federal Trade Comm'n,* Second Circuit, July 8,

1954.[59] It may easily raise problems of no small difficulty.

Another problem that has been growing in frequency is the inter-agency conflict. Each of these separate, largely independent, miniature governments has its own constituency, ambitions, and policies. Each has the human tendency to magnify its own jurisdiction, to practice what we call "empire building." Each tends more and more to collide with others and to bring their collision to the courts for settlement as a legal matter. There have been conflicts between the Interstate Commerce Commission and the Department of Justice, the Department of Agriculture and the Interstate Commerce Commission, and the Department of Justice and the Maritime Commission. These are difficult to settle as matters of law, for usually the law in general terms sets each agency on the course which conflicts with that of another. The legal paradox is dramatized by the fact that each agency is sometimes authorized to sue or defend in the name of the United States, so that we have the procedural absurdity of the United States suing itself. Where the one should yield to the other is a question which ought to be settled as a matter of policy, not law. But so far no mechanism exists for arbitrating these policy conflicts.

Such conflicts may catch the citizen in most difficult and unfair positions. Let us say the Internal Revenue Service rules that a particular product is oleomargarine and must be labeled as such and taxed accordingly. The Food and Drug Administration says that it is not oleomargarine and is mislabeled and proceeds to demand the penalty. Or let us say the Internal Revenue Service rules that a particular concern is entitled to deduct certain salaries for tax purposes, but the Federal Power Commission decides that the concern cannot treat those salaries as legitimate expenditures for rate-fixing purposes. It seems rather clearly the function and duty of Congress to resolve these inter-agency conflicts on the basis of policy rather than to leave them to the courts on the pretense that they are questions of law.

The administrative tribunals clearly are here to stay and probably to increase in number and powers. The values affected by their decisions probably exceed every year many times the dollar value of all money judgments rendered by the federal courts. They also affect vital rights of the citizen. There have been instances of excessive zeal and abuse of power. The same may be said of the judiciary. My own belief is that every safeguard should be thrown about the process of administrative adjudication so that its fact-finding will be honest, unprejudiced, neutral, and competent. It should be isolated from the prosecuting function. As a prosecutor, the body serves a constituency and promotes an interest. As a judge, it should know no constituent and serve no interest except justice. But in time we shall see these defects in the administrative process corrected, and the process will help supply the shortcomings we have found in the three original branches.

Perhaps our review has shown how unsettled is all that you thought to be immutable. But it was long ago said, "The science of government is the most abstruse of all sciences; if, indeed, that can be called a science which has but few fixed principles, and practically consists in little more than the exercise of a sound discretion, applied to the exigencies of the state as they arise. It is the science of experiment."[60]

III

THE SUPREME COURT

as a Political Institution

F EW accusations against the Supreme Court are made with more heat and answered with less candor than that it makes political decisions. Of course, the line between political science and legal science is not fixed and varies with one's definition of his terms. Any decision that declares the law under which a people must live or which affects the powers of their institutions is in a very real sense political. I have previously quoted Judge Cardozo, who contrasted the New York Court of Appeals and the United States Supreme Court in

these terms: "It [the New York Court of Appeals] is a
great common law court; its problems are lawyers' problems. But the Supreme Court is occupied chiefly with
statutory construction—which no man can make interesting—and with politics." [61] Of course, he used "politics" in no sense of partisanship but in the sense of pol-
icy-making. His remarks point to some features of the
federal judicial power which distinguish it from the
functions of the usual law court.

As already noted, the Constitutional Convention de-
liberately withheld from the Supreme Court power that
was political in form, such as a forthright power to veto
or revise legislation, and in that spirit the Court has
held itself without power to render advisory opinions
for the guidance even of the President. [62]

The Court has also observed a number of other self-
limitations which are intended to keep it out of active
participation in the political processes. It has refused
to inquire whether a state government complies with
the guarantee of a republican form of government [63] or
has properly ratified a proposed constitutional amendment. [64] It has given finality to the certification by the
other branches of government that a federal statute is
as signed, as against a claim of variance with the language actually adopted. [65] The duration of a state of
war, [66] the abrogation of treaties, [67] the recognition or
nonrecognition of foreign governments, [68] and matters
of foreign policy [69] generally, have been held to be political questions.

Even more controversial has been the effort to use the Supreme Court to control the districting of states for the elections of members of Congress,[70] to fix the terms on which a new political party may go on the state ballot,[71] and to abolish the "county unit" system used in some states.[72] Of course, it would be nice if there were some authority to make everybody do the things we ought to have done and leave undone the things we ought not to have done. But are the courts the appropriate catch-all into which every such problem should be tossed? One can answer "Yes" if some immediate political purpose overshadows concern for the judicial institution. But in most such cases interference by the Court would take it into matters in which it lacks special competence, let alone machinery of implementation.

The judicial power of the Supreme Court, however, does extend to all cases arising under the Constitution, to controversies to which the United States is a party, and to those between two or more states. Thus, the Court must face political questions in legal form, for surely a controversy between two separately organized political societies does present a political question, even if waged with the formalities of a lawsuit. And any decision which confirms, allocates, or shifts power as between different branches of the Federal Government or between it and a constituent state is equally political, no matter whether the decision be reached by a legislative or a judicial process. Our Constitution was the product and expression of a virile political philosophy held by those who wrote it. Controversies over its meaning often spring from political motives, for the object of politics always is to obtain power. Such controversies have to be solved either by consideration of the experiences and statements of the framers which indicate the original will, or by reference to some relevant subsequent events and currents of opinion deemed controlling. And all constitutional interpretations have political consequences.

We must not forget that, at bottom, the Civil War was fought over constitutional doctrine. It oversimplifies that tragedy to say that it was a war over slavery, an institution which many southern leaders had come to deplore and one which Mr. Lincoln did not propose to abolish in the states where it existed. The controversy was over the power of the Federal Government to control the spread of slavery into new territory, and over the voluntary or compulsory character of the federal compact. These, like most other questions which have deeply agitated our people, found their way to the Supreme Court in the guise of private controversies between litigating parties.

Only those heedless of legal history can deny that in construing the Constitution the Supreme Court from time to time makes new constitutional law or alters the law that has been. And it is idle to say that this is merely the ordinary process of interpretation, as in the law of negotiable instruments, for example. While a vast and respectable body of learning on the law of bills and notes existed in the Western World, the federal judiciary was not bound to apply it. The Supreme Court had even less jurisprudential guidance in solving its political or public law problems than in solving those of private law. The organic document itself was novel in phrase and philosophy, and there was no judicial experience and no very persuasive body of learning to aid in the interpretation of the instrument. True, the Privy Council in colonial times may have dealt with analogous controversies as to the *ultra vires* character of colonial acts, or as to the powers of colonial governments under Royal Charters. But in the original states the people appear to have been highly sensitive about the newly acquired position of each state as a sovereign power, won by the treaty which recognized their independence: as parties to the federal compact the states were not the equivalent of chartered colonial corporations. Small wonder, then, that Marshall's great constitutional decisions cite no precedents, that they are argued out of political philosophy, and that later courts again and again have overruled outmoded doctrines and turned to new ones as political or economic conditions changed.

The question that the present times put into the minds of thoughtful people is to what extent Supreme Court interpretations of the Constitution will or can preserve the free government of which the Court is a part. A cult of libertarian judicial activists now assails the Court almost as bitterly for renouncing power as the earlier "liberals" once did for assuming too much power. This cult appears to believe that the Court can find in a 4,000-word eighteenth-century document or its nineteenth-century Amendments, or can plausibly supply, some clear bulwark against all dangers and evils that today beset us internally. This assumes that the Court will be the dominant factor in shaping the constitutional practice of the future and can and will maintain, not only equality with the elective branches, but a large measure of supremacy and control over them. I may be biased against this attitude because it is so contrary to the doctrines of the critics of the Court, of whom I was one, at the time of the Roosevelt proposal to reorganize the judiciary. But it seems to me a doctrine wholly incompatible with faith in democracy, and in so far as it encourages a belief that the judges may be left to correct the result of public indifference to issues of liberty in choosing Presidents, Senators, and Representatives, it is a vicious teaching.

I shall pass over as not germane to my subject the question whether the Constitution itself is adequate for the security problems, the economic problems, and the political problems of our day. But I do not think that would be an academic question. We face the rivalry, which may break into the hostility, of concentrated governments that can decide quickly and secretly on their policies. Our power is so dispersed that nothing can be decided quickly or secretly. But I assume the permanence of our constitutional scheme, if for no other reason than our inability to agree on any other. The difficulties of amendment are such that many look to interpretation rather than amendment as a means of change.

But before we take the measure of the values the Court should and in some degree can protect, we must not overlook the things now practically beyond its control. Two of the greatest powers possessed by the political branches, which seem to me the disaster-potentials in our system, are utterly beyond judicial reach. These are the war power and the money, taxing, and spending power, which is the power of inflation. The improvident use of these powers can destroy the conditions for the existence of liberty, because either can set up great currents of strife within the population which might carry down constitutional forms and limitations before them.

The Constitution made what in its day was a logical division of the war power, delegating to Congress the power to declare war and to the President, as Commander in Chief, the power to conduct it. But the twentieth century ushered in an era of undeclared wars and thereby drained much of the substance out of the congressional power to declare war. It is apparent now that the President can so handle foreign affairs and the armed forces as to leave Congress no real choice but to declare war or as to involve us in warfare without any declaration. Korea stands as an example of the actual concentration of the war power in the President. That wars and rumors of wars are the great threats to political stability and to liberty needs no demonstration. Total

war means total subjection of the individual to the state.
We may resist "creeping socialism" or the coming of the
omnipotent socialized state in peacetime. But man-
power, labor, property, material, profit, rent, and even
food are subject to the planned economy and galloping
socialism of modern war. This form of military socializa-
tion is accepted as patriotic, and dissenters are coerced
into obedience. But it sets a pattern which is not easily
changed when peace is restored, and it is no accident
that the doctrines of Marx were sterile until the era of
total wars and then took their deepest root in countries
most deeply affected by war.

The other disaster-potential is the power over our
money system and the power to tax and spend for the
public welfare. In the famous Agricultural Adjustment
Act case the political branches lost a case and won a
cause. Even in holding that Act invalid, the Supreme
Court adopted the Federalist view of the spending
power and declared, "It results that the power of Congress to authorize expenditure of public moneys for
public purposes is not limited by the direct grants of
legislative power found in the Constitution."[73] The
Court earlier had held that a suit by a federal taxpayer
to restrain expenditures of public money on the ground
that the controlling statute is invalid cannot be main-
tained and that a state may not institute such an action
to protect her citizens.[74]

Thus the two disaster-potential powers are insulated
from all judicial control—the war power practically in

the hands of the President, the spending power in the hands of Congress. Either improvidently used can bring catastrophe so extensive as to carry down with it all else that we value. War and inflation and their kin have released the evil forces which have destroyed liberty elsewhere. No protection against these catastrophic courses can be expected from the judiciary. The people must guard against these dangers at the polls.

The political function which the Supreme Court, more or less effectively, may be called upon to perform comes to this: In a society in which rapid changes tend to upset all equilibrium, the Court, without exceeding its own limited powers, must strive to maintain the great system of balances upon which our free government is based. Whether these balances and checks are essential to liberty elsewhere in the world is beside the point; they are indispensable to the society we know. Chief of these balances are: first, between the Executive and Congress; second, between the central government and the states; third, between state and state; fourth, between authority, be it state or national, and the liberty of the citizen, or between the rule of the majority and the rights of the individual.

I have said that in these matters the Court must respect the limitations on its own powers because judicial usurpation is to me no more justifiable and no more promising of permanent good to the country than any other kind. So I presuppose a Court that will not depart from the judicial process, will not go beyond resolving

cases and controversies brought to it in conventional
form, and will not consciously encroach upon the functions of its coördinate branches. Whether in case of a
clearly unconstitutional usurpation of power by one of
the other branches the Court would be justified in step-
ping out of its judicial role and itself exercising a
usurped counterbalancing power, I do not stop to consider, because I think in such an event the judicial voice
would be little heeded in the chaos.

EXECUTIVE v. LEGISLATIVE

It is hard to conceive a task more fundamentally political than to maintain amidst changing conditions the
balance between the executive and legislative branches
of our federal system. The Supreme Court often is required to arbitrate between the two because litigation in
one form or another raises questions as to the legitimacy
of the acts of one branch or the other under the doctrine
of separation of powers. In such cases the Court has
found no precedent from any other country or in the
judicial interpretation of any similar written instrument, and it has had to devise its own doctrine from
time to time.

The Court, both before and after the Roosevelt influence was felt in its appointments, has tended strongly
to support the power of the President in matters involving foreign affairs.[75] On the other hand, where only
internal affairs are involved, the Court has been more
inclined to restrict executive power. It halted a presi-

dential effort indirectly to control the policies of the administrative agencies by removal of a Federal Trade Commissioner.[76] In the cases striking down the NIRA, the Court refused to sanction the congressional practice of delegating power to the President to make codes for industry that would be the equivalent of new laws.[77] The Court has kept the Executive from usurping the adjudicative function through military trials of offenders by holding such trials illegal in *Ex parte Milligan*, 4 Wall. (71 U.S.) 2, after, however, they had been running riot for a number of years. In the more recent case of *United States ex rel. Quirin* v. *Cox,* 317 U.S. 1, the Court met in special session to review the legality of the conviction of the eight German saboteurs who had been tried by a military commission set up by President Roosevelt, although his proclamation and order of July 2, 1942, provided that they should not be privileged "to seek any remedy or maintain any proceeding directly or indirectly, or to have any such remedy or proceeding sought on their behalf, in the courts. . . ."[78] This part of the President's proclamation was quietly rejected and the saboteurs were given a full hearing, as a result of which, however, the trial was found to have been legal and the convictions were sustained.

In the more recent Steel Seizure case[79] the Court refused to sanction a presidential seizure of private property without congressional authorization, holding that the President has no such inherent power under the Constitution. But I felt constrained in that case to point out the inadequacies of judicial power to appraise or control the realistic balance of power between Congress and the President.[80] This is because of the gap that exists between the President's paper powers and his actual powers. The real potency of the Executive office does not show on the face of the Constitution. The relative influence of the President and of the Congress has fluctuated widely, depending on the personal and political strength of the particular President as compared with that of the congressional leadership. A Congress stampeded by a powerful leader like Thaddeus Stevens may cripple a President who is politically vulnerable, and a senatorial coalition may break the foreign policy of even an able and strong President like Wilson. On the other hand, a White House tenant who is a skillful manipulator of his extralegal influences may force an unwelcome program through Congress.

What are these sources of presidential strength? First, the Executive power is concentrated in a single head in whose choice the whole nation has a part, making him the focus of public hopes and expectations. No collection of local representatives can rival him in prestige. None can gain such ready and effective access to the modern means of communication with the masses or exert such influence on public opinion; this is one of his most effective leverages upon those in Congress who are supposed to balance his power. As the nation's activities have spread, the President wields the power of appointment and promotion over a vast multitude of our people. He is not merely the Chief Magistrate of the Republic; he is the titular and usually the actual head of the prevailing political party, whose loyalties and interest enable him to win as political leader what he could not command under the Constitution. Woodrow Wilson summed it all up in the observation that "if he rightly interpret the national thought and boldly insist upon it, he is irresistible. . . . His office is anything he has the sagacity and force to make it." [81]

Yet it depends not upon the President alone but upon his sagacity and force measured against that of the Congress as manifested in its leadership. If Congress forfeits the respect of the country, it will not be able to balance the power of the Executive. No matter what the Supreme Court opines, only Congress itself can keep its power from slipping through its fingers.

FEDERAL POWER v. STATE POWER

It is the maintenance of the constitutional equilibrium between the states and the Federal Government that has brought the most vexatious questions to the Supreme Court. That it was the duty of the Court, within its own constitutional functions, to preserve this balance has been asserted by the Court many times; that the Constitution is vague and ambiguous on this subject is shown by the history preceding our Civil War. It is undeniable that ever since that war ended we have been in a cycle of rapid centralization, and Court opinions have sanctioned a considerable concentration of power

in the Federal Government with a corresponding dimi-
nution in the authority and prestige of state governments. Indeed, long ago an acute foreign observer
declared the United States to be "a nation concealed under the form of a federation." [82] As respected an authority as Charles Evans Hughes declared nearly three decades ago that "far more important to the development
of the country, than the decisions holding acts of Congress to be invalid, have been those in which the authority of Congress has been sustained and adequate national
power to meet the necessities of a growing country has
been found to exist within constitutional limitations." [83]

Here again the principal causes of this concentration
have not been within judicial control. Improved methods of transportation and communication; the increas-
ing importance of foreign affairs and of interstate commerce; the absorption of revenue sources by the nation
with the consequent appeal by distressed localities directly to Washington for relief and work projects, by-
passing the state entirely; the direct election of Senators;
and various other factors—all have contributed to move
the center of gravity from the state capital to that of the
nation.

I think it is a mistake to lump all states' rights together as is done so frequently in political discus-
sions.

There can be no doubt that in the original Constitution the states surrendered to the Federal Government
the power to regulate interstate commerce, or commerce
among the states. They did so in the light of a disastrous

experience in which commerce and prosperity were reduced to the vanishing point by states discriminating
against each other through devices of regulation, taxation and exclusion. It is more important today than it
was then that we remain one commercial and economic
unit and not a collection of parasitic states preying upon
each other's commerce. I make no concealment of and
offer no apology for my philosophy that the federal
interstate commerce power should be strongly supported and that the impingement of the states upon
that commerce which moves among them should be
restricted to narrow limits.

It was early perceived that to allow the Federal Government to spend money for internal improvements
would aggrandize its powers as against those of the states.
It was not until the famous decision holding the Social
Security Act constitutional that this controversy over
the federal power to tax and spend for the general welfare was settled, and settled in favor of the existence of
that power in the Federal Government.[84] I believe that
this controversy was rightly settled, but there is no deny-
ing that the power is vast and, uncontrolled, leads to
the invasion of sources of revenue and builds up the
Federal Government by creating organizations to make
the expenditures. But here we are dealing with powers
granted to the Federal Government, if not entirely without ambiguity, at least in language which fairly admits
of the construction given it and which fairly warned
those who adopted the Constitution that such results
might follow.

Considerations of a different nature arise from inter-
ferences with states' rights under the vague and ambiguous mandate of the Fourteenth Amendment. The legislative history of that Amendment is not enlightening,
and the history of its ratification is not edifying. I shall
not go into the controversy as to whether the Fourteenth Amendment, by a process of incorporation or
impregnation, directs against the states prohibitions
found in the earlier Amendments. Whether it does or
not, I think the Fourteenth Amendment has been con-
siderably abused.

For more than half a century the Supreme Court
found in the Fourteenth Amendment authority for
striking down various social experiments by the states.
The history of judicial nullification of state social and
economic legislation is too well known to justify repetition here. It came to its culmination when the Court
wound up the October 1935 Term by declaring that
there was no power in either state or nation to enact a
minimum wage law,[85] a position repudiated within a few
months by the conventions of both political parties and
retracted by the Court itself with some haste. That re-
traction probably brought an end to the use of the
Fourteenth Amendment to prevent experiments by the
states with economic and social and labor legislation.

The states have probably been more venturesome
and radical in their experimentation than the Congress.
This is perhaps explainable by the fact that their experi-

ments are more easily modified if unsuccessful. In the Granger movement and in the social legislation that followed it the states took the lead. On the other hand, they have enacted more extreme legislation for the control and restriction of labor unions when the tide ran the other way. In each instance the interest adversely affected has sought to obtain a holding that due process of law prevented the state from controlling its affairs and also prevented the nation from interfering, thus disabling either from exerting effective control. It is my basic view that whenever any organization or combination of individuals, whether in a corporation, a labor union or other body, obtains such economic or legal advantage that it can control or in effect govern the lives of other people, it is subject to the control of the Government, be it state or federal, for the Government can suffer no rivals in the field of coercion. Liberty requires that coercion be applied to the individual not by other individuals but by the Government after full inquiry into the justification.

Today, however, we have a different application of the Fourteenth Amendment. Today it is being used not to restrain state legislatures but to set aside the acts of state courts, particularly in criminal matters. This practice has proceeded to a point where the federal courts are in acute controversy with the state courts, and the assembled Chief Justices of the state courts have adopted severe resolutions condemning the federal intervention. I must say that I am rather in sympathy with the Chief Justices of the state courts on this subject. I believe we are unjustifiably invading the rights of the states by expanding the constitutional concept of due process to include the idea that the error of a trial court deprives it of "jurisdiction,"[86] by including in the concept by interpretation all other constitutional provisions not literally incorporated in the Fourteenth Amendment, and, in the alternative, by incorporating into it all of our ideas of decency, even to the point of making a constitutional issue of rulings upon evidence.

The Court has been drawing into the federal system more and more control by federal agencies over local police agencies. I have no doubt that the latter are often guilty of serious invasions of individual rights. But there are more fundamental questions involved in the interpretation of the antiquated, cumbersome, and vague civil rights statutes which give the Department of Justice the right to prosecute state officials.[87] If the Department of Justice must prosecute local officials, the FBI must investigate them, and no local agency which is subject to federal investigation, inspection, and discipline is a free agency. I cannot say that our country could have no central police without becoming totalitarian, but I can say with great conviction that it cannot become totalitarian without a centralized national police. At his trial Hermann Goering, with great candor, related the steps by which the Nazi party obtained com-

plete domination of Germany, and one of the first was
the establishment of the supremacy of the national over
the local police authorities. So it was in Russia, and so
it has been in every totalitarian state. All that is necessary is to have a national police competent to investigate all manner of offenses, and then, in the parlance
of the street, it will have enough on enough people, even
if it does not elect to prosecute them, so that it will find
no opposition to its policies. Even those who are supposed to supervise it are likely to fear it. I believe that
the safeguard of our liberty lies in limiting any national
policing or investigative organization, first of all to a
small number of strictly federal offenses, and secondly
to nonpolitical ones. The fact that we may have con-
fidence in the administration of a federal investigative
agency under its existing heads does not mean that it
may not revert again to the days when the Department
of Justice was headed by men to whom the investiga-
tory power was a weapon to be used for their own purposes.

It is a difficult question and always will remain a de-
batable question where, in particular instances, federal
due process should step into state court proceedings and
set them aside. When the state courts render harsh or
unconsidered judgments, they invite this power to be
used. But I think in the long run the transgressions of
liberty by the Federal Government, with its all-powerful
organization, are much more to be feared than those

of the several states, which have a greater capacity for
self-correction.

STATE v. STATE

Another clearly political type of litigation is that of
state against state. It was logical that in a federation
the different units should have some arbiter to settle
their differences. Congress was made a supervisor of their
separate compacts or agreements. The Supreme Court
was made the arbiter of their controversies. Here was
the precedent for an international court, for the states
waived their sovereignty sufficiently to submit to a compulsory jurisdiction over their controversies with each
other. This seems a hopeful precedent for an alternative to war and chaos and reprisals. Under this head of
jurisdiction the Court has settled boundary disputes,[88]
apportioned the debts of a divided state between the two
new divisions,[89] and determined many disputes over
rivers and waters.[90]

To what source may the Court look for law to govern such controversies? The actual practice perhaps is
well illustrated in Mr. Justice Cardozo's opinion in
New Jersey v. *Delaware*, 291 U.S. 361. His search carried him through many ancient documents, which he
interpreted according to the common law of property,
and he compared the claims of the two states in the light
of that body of learning. But this was inadequate for the
solution of the case and resort was had to international

law. He traced international law through the Court's own decisions and through all of the conventional authorities, American and foreign. He found international law inconclusive and no positive law applicable. He declared that "International law, or the law that governs between states, has at times, like the common law within states, a twilight existence during which it is hardly distinguishable from morality or justice, till at length the *imprimatur* of a court attests its jural quality."[91] He concluded that in these circumstances it was within the power of the judicial process to develop and apply a formula consonant with justice and with the political and social needs of the interstate or international legal system. Reduced to its simplest terms, what the Court seemed to be saying in that case was that it found no controlling law and was obliged to declare some, in the light of the experience and learning of the law in similar situations. The Court has no escape in many cases of this character from the undesirable alternatives of refusing to obey its duty to decide the case or of devising some rule of decision which has no precedent or positive law authority.

I know that it is now regarded as more or less provincial and reactionary to cite the Tenth Amendment, which reserves to the states and the people the powers not delegated to the Federal Government. That Amendment is rarely mentioned in judicial opinions, rarely cited in argument. But our forefathers made it a part of the Bill of Rights in order to retain in the localities certain powers and not to allow them to drift into centralized hands. Perhaps the Tenth Amendment is drifting into oblivion as constitutional provisions may sometimes do. That this can happen was illustrated recently when a lawyer friend asked me in a friendly way what I thought the Ninth Amendment to the Constitution meant. I vainly tried to recall what it was. I could not remember that in my long experience in government litigation I had ever made an argument based on the Ninth Amendment or that I had ever been obliged to meet one based thereon, and I could not recall ever having heard that Amendment mentioned by any Justice of the Court in conference or by any lawyer in an argument before it. So I turned to the work of my friends Hart and Wechsler, "The Federal Courts and the Federal System," and found that they had omitted the Ninth Amendment entirely from their printing of the important excerpts from the Constitution. Going to the full text, however, I found that it reads: "The enumeration in the Constitution, of certain rights, shall not be construed to deny or disparage others retained by the people." What are these other rights retained by the people? To what law shall we look for their source and definition? My lawyer friend kindly furnished me all the legislative history he had been able to find on the subject and called my attention to the only written commentary on it. But the Ninth Amendment rights which are not to be disturbed by the Federal Government are still a mystery to me.

MAJORITY v. INDIVIDUAL

Perhaps the most delicate, difficult and shifting of all balances which the Court is expected to maintain is that between liberty and authority. It is not so easy as some people believe to determine what serves liberty best by way of restriction of authority. For example, the removal of the Japanese from the West Coast during the War, which seemed to me plainly unconstitutional as applied to citizens, was rationalized as a service to ultimate liberty.[92] And I suppose no one would be more likely than Abraham Lincoln to win recognition by common vote as the greatest servant of freedom; yet President Lincoln, at the outset of his administration, suspended the writ of habeas corpus and resorted to wholesale arrest without warrant, detention without trial, and imprisonment without judicial conviction. Private mail was opened, and Cabinet officers simply sent telegrams ordering persons to be arrested and held without communication or counsel. The power was given to generals of various of the northern states to suppress newspapers and suspend the writ. President Lincoln, in his famous letter to Erastus Corning and others, defended his conduct, saying all that ever could be said and what always will be said in favor of such policies in time of emergency.[93] Those policies were sharply but unavailingly condemned in May of 1861 by the aged Chief Justice Taney, and he has said all that can be said on the other side.[94] Had Mr. Lincoln scrupulously observed the Taney policy, I do not know whether we would have had any liberty, and had the Chief Justice adopted Mr. Lincoln's philosophy as the philosophy of the law, I again do not know whether we would have had any liberty.

Lord Acton has said that liberty is a term of two hundred definitions.[95] About all I am sure of is that it is something never established for the future, but something which each age must provide for itself. I think we are given the rough outlines of a free society by our Bill of Rights. Liberty is not the mere absence of restraint, it is not a spontaneous product of majority rule, it is not achieved merely by lifting underprivileged classes to power, nor is it the inevitable by-product of technological expansion. It is achieved only by a rule of law.

But we must bear in mind that in the protection of individual or minority rights, we are often impinging on the principle of majority rule. Judicial opinions rarely face this dilemma. Let us take, for example, a community engaged largely in steel work, many of whose inhabitants are employed on night shifts and get their rest by day. Acting through regularly chosen representatives, the municipality duly enacts a regulation that precludes doorbell ringing in the distribution of literature or goods. A religious faction insists upon ringing doorbells to summon the occupant to the door to receive religious tracts that attack his religion and seek to convert him to the faith of the caller. If the Court holds that the right of free speech includes the right to enter upon private property and summon the owner to the door, it necessarily holds that a majority of a community are without the right to protect their hours of rest against such religiously inspired aggression.

In case after case in which so-called civil rights are involved, the question simmers down to one of the extent to which majority rule will be set aside. This issue has been debated,[96] but it has by no means been settled, and views shift as the occasion for judicial intervention shifts from case to case. About all we need to note, unless we were to go into a lengthy discussion of the particular cases of application of the power, is that the power of the Court to protect individual or minority rights has on the other side of the coin the power to restrain the majority. Some profound political philosophers, among them Mr. Jefferson, doubted the advisability of such intervention. Mr. Jefferson asked where else we may "find the origin of *just* powers, if not in the majority of the society? Will it be in the minority? Or in an individual of that minority?"[97] Perhaps we should say that it is only to be found in the law, in rationally and dispassionately devised rules which limit the majority's control over the individual and the minority. But even with the best draftsmanship possible such rules cannot but leave many questions for interpretation.

Moreover, we must remember that the Supreme Court is not the only force that is operating upon the Constitution. Custom, even in most vital matters, may serve to alter it. I suppose the election of a President is the most decisive and important recurring event in our national life. Nothing concerned the forefathers more, and they set up an elaborate and original system to assure non-partisan, deliberative choice from among all the citizens by electors selected for their leadership and judgment. This system has been suffocated by custom. The American public now sits at its television, entertained by the antics of two national conventions which limit their practicable choice of President to two men. Neither of these conventions nor the parties holding them has the slightest recognition in the Constitution, whose framers took every precaution to prevent the emergence of parties.

The Supreme Court, in the exercise of its power, has repeatedly come into collision with the strong executives of the nation. Jefferson, Jackson, Lincoln, and Franklin Roosevelt have been in open conflict with it. The clash has occurred where the Court was believed to be entering political realms through the passageway of private litigation. It would serve no purpose to review the merits of the conflict here, but in almost every instance it has occurred in such form as really to raise the question of minority and individual rights against majority rule: in each instance the President has been the representative of a powerful, popular majority. This is one of the great dilemmas of judicial power and one most avoided in discussion of the subject. So far as I can see, nothing has been accomplished in any of the controversies to settle or put at rest the questions which cause them. Judicial power to nullify a law duly passed by the representative process is a restriction upon the power of the majority to govern the country. Unrestricted majority rule leaves the individual in the minority unprotected. This is the dilemma and you have to take your choice. The Constitution-makers made their choice in favor of a limited majority rule.

In interpreting that limitation, of course, the Supreme Court from time to time makes and alters the law of the Constitution. It is idle to say that this is merely the ordinary process of private law interpretation. When the Court goes too far in interfering with the processes of the majority, it will again encounter a drive against its power or personnel. The power which has been exerted by the Court and which lies at the root of the controversies with the Executive has no more been renounced by the post-Roosevelt Court than it was by the pre-Roosevelt Court, though the lack of novel and progressive legislation has offered less occasion for its exercise. My philosophy has been and continues to be that such an institution, functioning by such methods, cannot and should not try to seize the initiative in shaping the policy of the law, either by constitutional interpretation or by statutory construction. While the line to be drawn between interpretation and legislation is difficult, and numerous dissents turn upon it, there is a limit beyond which the Court incurs the just charge of trying to supersede the law-making branches. Every Justice has been accused of legislating and every one has joined in that accusation of others. When the Court has gone too far, it has provoked reactions which have set back the cause it is designed to advance, and has sometimes called down upon itself severe rebuke.

If an organized society wants the kind of justice that an independent, professional judicial establishment is qualified to administer, our judiciary is certainly a most effective instrument for applying law and justice to individual cases and for cultivating public attitudes which rely upon law and seek justice. But I know of no modern instance in which any judiciary has saved a whole people from the great currents of intolerance, passion, usurpation, and tyranny which have threatened liberty and free institutions. The Dred Scott decision did not settle the question of the power to end slavery, and I very much doubt that had Mr. Justice McLean not dissented in that case it would have done any more to avoid war. No court can support a reactionary regime and no court can innovate or implement a new one. I doubt that any court, whatever its powers, could have saved Louis XVI or Marie Antoinette. None could have avoided the French Revolution, none could have stopped its excesses, and none could have prevented its culmination in the dictatorship of Napoleon. In Germany a courageous court refused to convict those whom the Nazi government sought to make the scapegoats for the Reichstag fire, clandestinely set by the Nazis themselves, and other courts decreed both the Nazi and the Communist parties to be illegal under German law. Those judgments fell on deaf ears and became dead letters because the political forces at the time were against them.

It is not idle speculation to inquire which comes first, either in time or importance, an independent and enlightened judiciary or a free and tolerant society. Must we first maintain a system of free political government to assure a free judiciary, or can we rely on an aggressive, activist judiciary to guarantee free government? While each undoubtedly is a support for the other, and the two are frequently found together, it is my belief that the attitude of a society and of its organized political forces, rather than its legal machinery, is the controlling force in the character of free institutions.

I am a fairly consistent reader of British newspapers. I have been repeatedly impressed with the speed and certainty with which the slightest invasion of British individual freedom or minority rights by officials of the government is picked up in Parliament, not merely by the opposition but by the party in power, and made the subject of persistent questioning, criticism, and sometimes rebuke. There is no waiting on the theory that the judges will take care of it. In this country, on the contrary, we rarely have a political issue made of any kind of invasion of civil liberty. On the contrary, district attorneys who have been rebuked by the courts are frequently promoted by the public. The attitude seems to be, leave it to the judges. Years after the event takes place, the judges make their pronouncement, often in the form of letting some admittedly guilty person go, and that ends the matter. In Great Britain, to observe civil liberties is good politics and to transgress the rights of the individual or the minority is bad politics. In the United States, I cannot say that this is so. Whether the political conscience is relieved because the responsibility here is made largely a legal one, I cannot say, but of this I am sure: any court which undertakes by its legal processes to enforce civil liberties needs the support of an enlightened and vigorous public opinion which will be intelligent and discriminating as to what cases really are civil liberties cases and what questions really are involved in those cases. I do not think the American public is enlightened on this subject.

Sometimes one is tempted to quote his former self, not only to pay his respects to the author but to demonstrate the consistency of his views, if not their correctness. On the 150th anniversary of the Supreme Court, speaking for the executive branch of the Government as Attorney General, I said to the Justices:

"However well the Court and its bar may discharge their tasks, the destiny of this Court is inseparably linked to the fate of our democratic system of representative government. Judicial functions, as we have evolved them, can be discharged only in that kind of society which is willing to submit its conflicts to adjudication and to subordinate power to reason. The future of the Court may depend more upon the competence of the executive and legislative branches of government to solve their problems adequately and in time than upon the merit which is its own."[98]

NOTES

NOTES

Notes preceded by an asterisk (*) were not supplied
by Mr. Justice Jackson.

1. They are traceable to the *jus gentium* of the Roman jurists
and the teachings of Cicero. A century before our Revolution,
Pufendorf at Heidelberg occupied a chair as professor of the law
of nature and nations. Edward S. Corwin, *Liberty against Government,* ch. ii (1948). [This note was written by Mr. Justice Jackson
except for the *Corwin* citation.]

2. Bryce says the doctrine which for nearly two thousand years
was a "harmless maxim, almost a commonplace of morality," suddenly became dynamite which shattered ancient monarchies and
shook Europe. Bryce, II *Studies in History and Jurisprudence,*
599 (*c.* 1901).

Acton refers to "American ideas, sufficient to subvert every
European state" being transplanted into France. Lord Acton,
"The American Revolution," in *Lectures on Modern History,*
edited by John N. Figgis and Reginald V. Laurence, p. 313 (Lon-
don, 1906). [This note was written by Mr. Justice Jackson except
for the citations.]

3. Mathiot, *France,* 54 COL. L. REV. 765, 766.

4. *Dennis* v. *United States,* 341 U.S. 494, 561 (concurring opinion).

5. See Harris, *Tyranny on Trial* (1954).

*6. See generally Camus, *The Rebel* (1954). [Mr. Justice Jackson had written the word "Camus" next to this note.]

*7. See Warren, II *The Supreme Court in United States His-
tory,* 420-423, 517-519 (1935); Hearings before the Senate Committee on the Judiciary on S. 1392, 75th Cong., 1st Sess., 11-13,
25, 40-41, 44, 1913, 2011-2012.

*8. 15 Stat. 44; *Ex Parte McCardle,* 7 Wall. (74 U.S.) 506. See also Creation of the Federal Judiciary, Sen. Doc. 91, 75th Cong., 1st Sess., 269-273 (1938).

*9. Beveridge, IV *The Life of John Marshall*, 551 (*c.* 1919).

*10. II *Papers of James Madison*, 733-734, 783-791 (Gilpin ed. 1840).

*11. E.g., III *Correspondence and Public Papers of John Jay*, pp. 486-489 (*c.* 1891); *Hayburn's Case*, 2 Dall. (2 U.S.) 409; *Muskrat* v. *United States*, 219 U.S. 346; *Alabama* v. *Arizona*, 291 U.S. 286; *Keller* v. *Potomac Electric Power Co.*, 261 U.S. 428.

*12. E.g., *United States* v. *Alaska S.S. Co.*, 253 U.S. 113; *Alabama State Federation of Labor* v. *McAdory*, 325 U.S. 450; *United Public Workers of America* v. *Mitchell*, 330 U.S. 75.

*13. See pp. 54-55 and notes 64-72, *infra*.

*14. Cardozo, *The Nature of the Judicial Process* (1921).

*15. E.g., *Rescue Army* v. *Municipal Court*, 331 U.S. 549, 575-585; *International Brotherhood of Teamsters, Chauffeurs, Warehousemen & Helpers Union* v. *Denver Milk Producers, Inc.*, 334 U.S. 809.

*16. E.g., *Ricaud* v. *American Metal Co.*, 246 U.S. 304, 307; *Elwell* v. *Fosdick*, 134 U.S. 500; *Alton* v. *Alton*, 347 U.S. 610.

*17. I Warren, *op. cit.*, 653-655. Morgan, *Justice William Johnson, The First Dissenter*, 168-169, 171, 172, 183-185 (1954). [Mr. Justice Jackson had read the proofs of the Morgan book.]

18. Hughes, *The Supreme Court of the United States*, 68 (1928).

19. Cardozo, *Law and Literature*, 14 YALE REV. 699, 715 (1925).

*20. *Dred Scott* v. *Sandford*, 19 How. (60 U.S.) 393.

*21. Frankfurter and Landis, *The Business of the Supreme Court*, 82-83, 98-101 (1927); Hearings before the Senate Committee on the Judiciary on S. 1392, 75 Cong., 1st Sess., p. 1871.

*22. Letter from Chief Justice Hughes to Senator Burton K. Wheeler, Senate Report No. 711, 75th Cong., 1st Sess., p. 40.

*23. 54 Stat. 670, 671, 18 U.S.C. (1946 ed.) § 11; *Dennis* v. *United States*, 341 U.S. 494.

*24. 54 Stat. 670, 673, 8 U.S.C. (1946 ed.) § 137; *Harisiades* v. *Shaughnessy*, 342 U.S. 580.

*25. *Joint Anti-Fascist Refugee Committee* v. *McGrath*, 341 U.S. 123.

*26. E.g., *Massachusetts* v. *Mellon*, 262 U.S. 447; see *United States* v. *Realty Co.*, 163 U.S. 427; *Cincinnati Soap Co.* v. *United States*, 301 U.S. 308.

*27. E.g., *United States* v. *Curtiss-Wright Export Corp.*, 299 U.S. 304; see *United States* v. *Belmont*, 301 U.S. 324; *Chicago & Southern Air Lines, Inc.* v. *Waterman S.S. Corp.*, 333 U.S. 103.

*28. E.g., *Selective Draft Law Cases*, 245 U.S. 366; *Lichter* v. *United States*, 334 U.S. 742.

29. E.g., *Korematsu* v. *United States*, 323 U.S. 214.

*30. 1 Stat. 73.

31. Bryce, I *American Commonwealth*, 29 (1893).

32. *The Peoples Ancient and Just Liberties Reasserted in the Digest of the Tryal of William Penn, and William Mead*, 11 (private printing 1954).

*33. 304 U.S. 64, 78.

*34. *Hinderlider* v. *La Plata River Co.*, 304 U.S. 92, 110.

35. E.g., *Clearfield Trust Co.* v. *United States*, 318 U.S. 363; *D'Oench, Duhme & Co.* v. *Federal Deposit Insurance Corp.*, 315 U.S. 447.

*36. §§ 11, 12, 13, 25, 1 Stat. 78-81, 85.

*37. James, *A List of Legal Treatises Printed in the British Colonies and the American States before 1801*, HARVARD LEGAL ESSAYS 159 (1934).

*38. 304 U.S., at 74.

*39. 304 U.S., at 80.

*40. E.g., *Meredith* v. *Winter Haven*, 320 U.S. 228; *Guttmann* v. *Illinois Central R. Co.*, 189 F.2d 927; *Springfield* v. *Carter*, 175 F.2d 914; *Adam Hat Stores, Inc.* v. *Lefco*, 134 F.2d 101; *Crab Orchard Improvement Co.* v. *Chesapeake & Ohio R. Co.*, 115 F.2d 277.

*41. E.g., *Fidelity Union Trust Co.* v. *Field*, 311 U.S. 169; *Six Companies of California* v. *Joint Highway District*, 311 U.S. 180; *West* v. *American Telephone & Telegraph Co.*, 311 U.S. 223; *Stoner* v. *New York Life Insurance Co.*, 311 U.S. 464.

*42. Rule 19 (1) (b), 346 U.S. 967.

*43. On the subject of water rights generally, see *United States* v. *Gerlach Live Stock Co.*, 339 U.S. 725.

*44. 1 Stat. 122.

*45. *Rice v. Rice*, 336 U.S. 674.

*46. E.g., *Thormann v. Frame*, 176 U.S. 350; *Burbank v. Ernst*, 232 U.S. 162; *Worcester County Trust Co. v. Riley*, 302 U.S. 292, 299; *Riley v. New York Trust Co.*, 315 U.S. 343.

*47. *Texas v. Florida*, 306 U.S. 398.

*48. E.g., *Order of United Commercial Travelers of America v. Wolfe*, 331 U.S. 586; *Pink v. A.A.A. Highway Express, Inc.*, 314 U.S. 201; *Broderick v. Rosner*, 294 U.S. 629; *New York Life Insurance Co. v. Head*, 234 U.S. 149.

*49. E.g., *Bradford Electric Light Co. v. Clapper*, 286 U.S. 145; *Cardillo v. Liberty Mutual Insurance Co.*, 330 U.S. 469; *Industrial Comm'n v. McCartin*, 330 U.S. 622; *Pacific Employers Insurance Co. v. Industrial Accident Comm'n*, 306 U.S. 493.

*50. *Wells v. Simonds Abrasive Co.*, 345 U.S. 514.

*51. See Jackson, *Full Faith and Credit* (1945).

*52. *Administrative Management in the Government of the United States* (Report of the President's Committee on Administrative Management 1937), 36.

*53. 81 Cong. Rec. 188.

*54. 86 Cong. Rec. 13942.

55. *Crowell v. Benson*, 285 U.S. 22.

*56. See generally, Schwartz, *French Administrative Law and the Common-Law World* (1954). See also Dicey, *Law of the Constitution*, ch. xii (9th ed. 1939); Uhler, *Review of Administrative Acts*, 14-16, 31 (Michigan Legal Studies 1942). [Mr. Justice Jackson had indicated that he would cite the Schwartz book.]

*57. Cf. *Ellis v. Interstate Commerce Comm'n*, 237 U.S. 434; *Federal Trade Comm'n v. American Tobacco Co.*, 264 U.S. 298; *Jones v. Securities & Exchange Comm'n*, 298 U.S. 1, with *Oklahoma Press Publishing Co. v. Walling*, 327 U.S. 186; *Shapiro v. United States*, 335 U.S. 1; *United States v. Morton Salt Co.*, 338 U.S. 632.

*58. *Humphrey's Executor v. United States*, 295 U.S. 602.

*59. This case has since been reported at 214 F.2d 338.

60. *Anderson v. Dunn*, 6 Wheat. (19 U.S.) 204, 226.

*61. The statement was a personal one made to Mr. Justice

Jackson and is recorded in Jackson, *Full Faith and Credit*, p. 2 (1945).

*62. See pp. 11-12 and n. 11, *supra*.

*63. E.g., *Cochran* v. *Louisiana State Board*, 281 U.S. 370; *Mountain Timber Co.* v. *Washington*, 243 U.S. 219; *Pacific States Telephone & Telegraph Co.* v. *Oregon*, 223 U.S. 118.

*64. E.g., *Coleman* v. *Miller*, 307 U.S. 433; *Leser* v. *Garnett*, 258 U.S. 130; *Luther* v. *Borden*, 7 How. (48 U.S.) 1.

*65. E.g., *Field* v. *Clark*, 143 U.S. 649; *Harwood* v. *Wentworth*, 162 U.S. 547; *Flint* v. *Stone Tracy Co.*, 220 U.S. 107, 143.

*66. E.g., *Ludecke* v. *Watkins*, 335 U.S. 160; *Commercial Trust Co.* v. *Miller*, 262 U.S. 51. Cf. *Woods* v. *Cloyd W. Miller Co.*, 333 U.S. 138, 146 (concurring opinion).

*67. E.g., *Clark* v. *Allen*, 331 U.S. 503; *Terlinden* v. *Ames*, 184 U.S. 270; *Doe* v. *Braden*, 16 How. (57 U.S.) 635.

*68. E.g., *United States* v. *Pink*, 315 U.S. 203; *Oetjen* v. *Central Leather Co.*, 246 U.S. 297; *Kennett* v. *Chambers*, 14 How. (55U.S.) 38.

*69. E.g., *Harisiades* v. *Shaughnessy*, 342 U.S. 580; *Chicago & Southern Air Lines, Inc.* v. *Waterman S.S. Corp.*, 333 U.S. 103; *In re Cooper*, 143 U.S. 472; *Foster* v. *Neilson*, 2 Pet. (27 U.S.) 253.

*70. E.g., *Wood* v. *Broom*, 287 U.S. 1; *Colegrove* v. *Green*, 328 U.S. 549; *Anderson* v. *Jordan*, 343 U.S. 912.

*71. E.g., *MacDougall* v. *Green*, 335 U.S. 281; *Illinois ex rel. Sankstone* v. *Jarecki*, 346 U.S. 861; *White* v. *Howard*, 347 U.S. 910.

*72. E.g., *Cook* v. *Fortson*, *Turman* v. *Duckworth*, 329 U.S. 675; *South* v. *Peters*, 339 U.S. 276.

73. *United States* v. *Butler*, 297 U.S. 1, 66.

74. *Massachusetts* v. *Mellon*, 262 U.S. 447.

75. E.g., *United States* v. *Curtiss-Wright Export Corp.*, 299 U.S. 304; *Chicago & Southern Air Lines, Inc.* v. *Waterman S.S. Corp.*, 333 U.S. 103.

76. *Humphrey's Executor* v. *United States*, 295 U.S. 602.

77. *Panama Refining Co.* v. *Ryan*, 293 U.S. 388; *A.L.A. Schechter Poultry Corp.* v. *United States*, 295 U.S. 495.

*78. Proclamation 2561, 7 Fed. Reg. 5101.

79. *Youngstown Sheet & Tube Co.* v. *Sawyer*, 343 U.S. 579.

*80. *Id.,* at 634 (concurring opinion).

81. Wilson, *Constitutional Government in the United States,* 68, 69 (1911).

82. Dicey, *Law of the Constitution,* App. 604. (9th ed. 1939).

83. Hughes, *The Supreme Court of the United States,* 96 (1928).

84. *Helvering* v. *Davis,* 301 U.S. 619.

*85. *Morehead* v. *New York ex rel. Tipaldo,* 298 U.S. 587.

*86. *Johnson* v. *Zerbst,* 304 U.S. 458, 467-468; see also *Brown* v. *Allen,* 344 U.S. 443, 532 (concurring opinion). [Mr. Justice Jackson had written *"Johnson"* next to this note.]

87. See *Screws* v. *United States,* 325 U.S. 91.

*88. E.g., *Maryland* v. *West Virginia,* 217 U.S. 1; *Indiana* v. *Kentucky,* 163 U.S. 520; *Missouri* v. *Iowa,* 7 How. (48 U.S.) 660.

*89. *Virginia* v. *West Virginia,* 206 U.S. 290.

*90. E.g., *New Jersey* v. *Delaware,* 291 U.S. 361; *Wisconsin* v. *Illinois,* 278 U.S. 367; *Kansas* v. *Colorado,* 206 U.S. 46.

*91. 291 U.S., at 383.

92. *Korematsu* v. *United States,* 323 U.S. 214.

*93. VIII *Complete Works of Abraham Lincoln* (ed. Nicolay and Hay), 298 (c. 1894).

*94. *Ex parte Merryman,* Reports of Cases at Law and Equity and in the Admiralty determined in the Circuit Court of the United States for the District of Maryland by Roger Brooke Taney, 246 (1871).

*95. Acton, *Essays on Freedom and Power,* 14 (1948).

96. *West Virginia State Board of Education* v. *Barnette,* 319 U.S. 624.

*97. Letter to Major John Cartwright, June 5, 1824, VII *Writings of Thomas Jefferson* (ed. Washington), 356 (1861).

98. 309 U.S. v, vii.